Traditional Dress

Knowledge and Methods of Old-Time Clothing

Revised Edition

Traditional Dress
Knowledge and Methods of Old-Time Clothing

Revised Edition

Adolf Hungrywolf

Native Voices

Summertown, Tennessee

Copyright 2003 by Adolf Hungrywolf
Cover design by Warren Jefferson
Book design by Jerry Lee Hutchens

Native Voices
Book Publishing Company
P.O. Box 99
Summertown, TN 38483
1-888-260-8458
www.bookpubco.com

04 03 02 01   1 2 3 4

ISBN 1-57067-147-8

Hungrywolf, Adolf.
  Traditional dress : knowledge and methods of old-time clothing / Adolf
Hungrywolf.
      p. cm.
    ISBN 1-57067-147-8
  1. Indians of North America--Clothing. I. Title.

E98.C8H78 2003
646.4'0089'97--dc21
                                        2003001428

Cover: Wa-Kon-Kon-Wa-La-Son-Me, known in English as Umapine, chief of the Cayuse tribe of northern Oregon. He was photographed in his finest traditional dress at the famous Last Great Council of Chiefs, held near the Crow Reservation in 1909. At that time he said:

> "I have come from the far distant mountains . . . to meet the chiefs in council . . . We each have two hands, two feet, two eyes, two ears, but one nose, one mouth, one head, and one heart. We all breathe the same air; we are all, therefore, brothers . . .

> "It was the custom among my people to narrate to their children the history of the past and they narrated to me that my tribe had learned to make clothing from furs which were gotten from Animals, and this clothing was comfortable during the winter time as well as in the summer. There is still some of this clothing remaining among older Indians of my tribe . . . The white man's clothing is fit for men to wear. I like to wear his clothes very well, but I also like to wear the clothing my people used to wear in the olden time.

> "I have respect for any kind of people . . . The only difference between myself and the white man is that his complexion is lighter than mine."

Title page: "Pahsetopah, Osage Indian, in Full Dress, Oklahoma." For many decades this has been the stereotype image of an American Indian chief, with buckskin fringed suit and a long trailing headdress of eagle feathers. For some tribes this look was indeed traditional for their leaders, while many other tribes simply adopted it in order to be more acceptable to society at large. Those leaders qualified to dress like this are generally not pleased when others of their people put on such clothes just for show, without being qualified. This holds even more true when Native leaders see non-natives dressed in such clothing, sometimes even calling themselves chiefs.

About the photographs in this book:

As a third generation photographer I've enjoyed collecting old photos since I was a boy, besides taking and developing my own, My special interests have been photo scenes of the "Old West," particularly those showing rains and railroading, and those of Native People and their cultural lives. I've used both kinds in most of my books.

Years ago it was possible to find old photos at swap meets and garage sales for pennies, or by the box and album full at auctions and antique shows, often for just a few dollars. Unfortunately, most old photos have very little information written on them—often none at all. Besides gathering up such photos for over 40 years, I've also enjoyed the detective work required to find out what and who they show. On these pages are some of the results.

Adolf Hungrywolf

Contents

Introduction

The Native American People, back in the Old Days, dressed according to tribal tradition and personal desire. Like everything else in their lives, appearance was dictated foremost by Visions and Dreams. Sometimes a totally new article or method came about this way—often with spiritual meaning that was respected and not copied by others. More often, however, the Visions of personal appearance were based on pleasing articles and methods that the individual had seen previously on another tribe member, on a member of another tribe, or even on a person from some other culture. For instance, it is believed that many intricate geometric beadwork designs were inspired by similar designs on Oriental rugs that were brought into the frontier country by white settlers. Again, the famed "war bonnet" was used originally by the Sioux tribe—and a few neighbors—to distinguish warriors who had accomplished enough brave deeds that their representative eagle feathers could be made up into a headdress. The style and meaning of the bonnet was adopted by numerous tribes during the latter part of the 19th century. By the beginning of the present century, no Native dress was considered complete without a war bonnet. So virtually every tribe adopted the style, and the traditional bonnet all but lost its meaning.

The Native People in the Old Days certainly placed as much pride in their personal appearance as any group of people ever have. Their dress consisted of handmade clothing, necklaces of natural materials or wonderful, prized beads, little bunches of feathers and furs worn here and there, hats made of skins—each thing with a story behind it that was sure to recall some prior happy moments at discouraging times.

The following presentation is meant to inspire your thoughts about personal appearance. It does not give step-by-step instructions for weekend diversion. Rather, it gathers together some old styles and some old methods, with the hope that you will be tempted to gather the materials at your disposal and make some of the items to suit your own personal thoughts and way of life.

The people of some North American tribes maintained their distinct dressing styles well into the 1900s. This photo shows such an example, taken by a studio photographer in Calgary around 1910. It shows Jonas Dixon, a young Stoney man, with his wife. Both are dressed in their finest clothing for this portrait session. She has on a woolen dress, a white canvas apron, a fringed and plaid Scottish shawl, and a flowered scarf. He wears fully beaded moccasins, a fringed pair of smoked buckskin leggings, a long breechcloth decorated with many colors of ribbons, a decorated shirt and cloth vest, and a dance roach of porcupine and deer hair on his head. The bead bandolier bag over his shoulder is decorated with weasels and other animal skins that represented the sacred powers of his dreams, which came from his outdoor life. Around his neck is a conch shell choker with a necklace of deerhorn tips, made in imitation of grizzly claws. When Jonas Dixon gave me this photo of himself in 1975, he had on a pair of faded jeans, work boots, and a flannel shirt. He said it was easy in his young days to go around dressed traditionally, because many of his Stoney People still did, partly because there weren't a lot of strangers in their country then.

The Old Ways of Dressing

"It has always been observed that all the various tribes have a close resemblance in their dress: that of the North Americans in their original state, consists entirely of furs and hides, one piece is fastened round the waist, which reaches the middle of the thigh, and another larger piece is thrown over the shoulders. Their stockings are of skins, fitted to the shape of the leg: the seams are ornamented with Porcupines' quills: their shoes are of the skin of the Deer, Elk, or Buffalo, dressed, for the most part with the hair on, they are made to fasten about the ankles, where they have ornaments of brass or tin, about an inch long, hung by thongs. The women are all covered from the knees upward. Their shifts cover their bodies, but not the arms. Their petticoats reach from the waist to the knees: and both are of leather. Their shoes and stockings are not different from those of the men. Those men who wish to appear gay pluck the hairs from their heads, except a round spot of about two inches diameter on the crown of the head; on this are fastened plumes of feathers with quills of ivory or silver. The peculiar ornaments of this part are the distinguishing marks of the different nations. They some-times paint their faces black, but more often red, they bore their noses and slit their ears, and in both they wear various orna-ments. The higher ranks of women dress their hair sometimes with silver in a peculiar manner; they sometimes paint it. They have generally a large spot of paint near the ear, on each side of the head, and not unfrequently a small spot on the brow. These People, it is true, have made several improvements in their dresses, since they commenced to receive European commodities."

So wrote John McIntosh in the 1840s in his book, *The Origin of the North American Indians*. The manner of dressing had already been quite affected among some of the Eastern tribes by their contact with the new cultures

Chief Louison was an old and respected leader of the Salish-Flathead People in Montana around 1910, when he was photographed inside his tipi with some of his best traditional dress. The eagle feather headdress was for him a fairly new symbol of leadership, adopted from the Sioux and other Plains tribes. His feather-covered shield is a reminder of his younger days as a brave and noted warrior. Although he wears just a striped cloth shirt and black vest, behind him hangs his ceremonial outfit, including a weasel-decorated headdress and suit, the double trailer for his eagle bonnet, a pair of long straps with dance bells, and a plume-decorated reservation hat. On the ground behind him is a traditional rawhide parfleche for storage.

when McIntosh wrote. The spectacular dress of the People of the Plains and many of their neighbors was then beginning to go through a period of changes that reached an artistic climax during the following fifty years. In that period, the People took advantage of the many new materials available from traders to make and design articles that were inspired by their spiritual past and their still-natural lives.

You are like the People of that period. You can take advantage of the multitudes of materials and tools that are available today to make and design articles inspired by your spiritual knowledge of the past and your opportunity to seek a natural life in the present. Be proud of your person—take pride in the appearance of your body and the manner of your dress. Seek beauty in everyone, and let everyone appreciate the beauty in you.

The everyday clothing worn by this Sarcee (Tsu-tinaa) couple is easy to make by hand with basic materials. Included are leather moccasins, cotton dress and shirt, leggings, breechcloth, and the woman's blanket, all made of wool. Her head-band is a fur strip, while he wears bits of fur tied to his braids, both proba-bly having sacred meanings as with the big round shell at his neck, which usually represents the Sun. His large rawhide knife sheath is decorated with a lot of brass tacks pounded in neatly, the pointed ends then clipped off. The photo was taken near the Rocky Mountains, west of Calgary, Alberta, in the 1890s by C. W. Mathers.

12

Introduction to Sewing

Most anything is easy to sew by hand, as long as you use common sense. Patience is the most difficult requirement. Anyone can produce fine work who has the patience to take short, even, and tight stitches.

Tools

In the old days the only tools for sewing were a knife for cutting, an awl of pointed bone for making holes, and strips of sinew to sew the materials together with. For inspiration, as well as for appearance of certain items (such as Medicine bags), nothing is better than the old-time process. You separate the piece of sinew into strips of the thickness required for the project. Soak one of the strips in your mouth until it becomes soft and workable. Then draw it across your lap with your left hand, from right to left, at the same time rolling your other hand over the strip with a downward motion. Thus twisted, the strip is poked through the awl holes and pulled tight. Leave the end used for poking dry and untwisted, so that it will be stiff and hard, like the rest of the strip when it dries. Sinew sewing is tedious, and beginning attempts are often clumsy. For making practical clothing you would do well to keep in mind the efforts of the past, while proceeding with the methods that follow.

The basic sewing tools of today are the needle and thread. Scissors, wax, and thimble are almost as important. A few dollars will buy a lifetime supply of all these materials in any department store that carries notions.

A dime-store package of assorted needles will take care of most sewing needs. Large needles are easier to handle and will take rougher treatment without bending or breaking. Smaller needles are easier to push through the material. Three-cornered needles are particularly good for leather sewing. When sewing leather, try to use the smallest practical needle—one with an eye just big enough to take your thread—or you will be struggling to push each stitch through. An awl is a handy tool to use when tough leather is being sewn. Perforate a number of holes with it and then follow with the needle and thread. A sharpened ice pick works well as an awl.

Thread should always be at least as tough as the material you are sewing. A good standard type is made of nylon. This comes in tiny rolls, as well as mile-long spools, and is virtually unbreakable. Use it doubled for extra strength and rigidity.

Scissor types are many; the most important factor to consider about them is sharpness. You will wear out patience and hands with dull scissors, and your work is likely to look ragged besides. Get a good pair of scissors that will keep a sharp edge, and have them sharpened once in awhile. Scissors will cut cloth and most leather. For tough leather, it is better to use a ruler and a razor blade. For fur, use a razor blade and cut on the skin side to avoid damaging the hair.

If you've ever perforated your fingertip with the fat end of a needle that you were attempting to push through thick material, then you will appreciate the value of a thimble. Learn to handle the needle with your thumb and middle finger, so that your index (or thimble) finger will always be free to give that helpful boost once your needle has found its mark. Buy a good-fitting thimble—too loose or too tight will distract your efforts at smooth sewing.

Pulling your length of thread back and forth over a small piece of beeswax will greatly improve the appearance and effort of your sewing. It will eliminate the slippery feeling of your thread and allow your stitches to remain snug after you pull them tight.

Sewing Methods

Hand-sewn items are generally stitched up inside out. When the completed item is turned right side out, the stitches should be barely visible between the even seam. These stitches can be hidden altogether if a thin strip of material is sewn between the two main layers and the stitches are kept quite firm. Sometimes a strip of contrasting material is used this way, with very pleasing results. Red wool cloth, for instance, makes a beautiful "well" between leather seams. Fur strips look very nice when used as welts between pieces of heavy wool material.

After you have made a wrapping paper pattern of your proposed work and then cut out your actual material (allowing ¼ inch for the seams), line up and pin the whole piece along the seams with stick pins. This will help keep your work properly lined up and will counter the stretching that your material may do while you are sewing. Two-piece items that are to be sewn most or all of the way around (such as pouches and two-piece moccasins) should be begun in the center and sewn first down one side, then the other—again, to outwit the material's tendency to stretch and end up lopsided.

Fasten your thread to the material either by knotting the end or by leaving a tail, taking several close stitches, and then tying a double knot with the tail and the main thread. Knotted ends alone tend to pull out during use. The basic stitch for sewing material inside out is the simple overhand (or loop) stitch. Again, keep the stitches even and tight, and sew close enough to the edge of the material to avoid unsightly and large stitches from showing when right side out (but not so close that pressure from use will rip the stitches through the material). At the end of a seam, or when running out of thread, either of the methods for tying thread may again be used. Waxing the end of the thread and taking a half dozen close, tight stitches is often sufficient for the end of sewing.

LOOP STITCH &
STARTING KNOT

WELT

Materials

A few comments may be worthwhile here. If you buy your material, get the best you can afford. Endless hours of careful sewing will be wasted if your material shrinks, tears, or pulls out of shape. The best deals on cloth can generally be found in thrift stores and in the remnant selections of quality clothing manufacturers. Taxidermists often sell unclaimed, tanned hides for a fair price. They may also have a wide selection of furs available, while thrift stores will sell used fur pieces even cheaper.

Buckskin (the common name given to tanned deer hides) is the best all-around leather for clothing. It is extremely tough and durable, yet soft, and easy to cut and sew. The money you save by buying cheap, commercial "splits" is nothing when compared to the stiff, uncomfortable piece you may end up with. The feel of new leather does not change much for the better with age, so buy accordingly.

Rawhide for clothing—don't embarrass yourself by asking for it. A rawhide is just what the name implies—an untanned hide. You would do as well to make your clothing from plywood sheets.

If money is no object, then buy deer, elk, or moose hides that have been tanned by Reservation People. Sold as "Indian-tanned" hides, this kind of leather is expensive and hard to find, but feels smooth and soft like velvet. If you buy it "smoked," it will have a nice brown color, an aroma you will never forget, and will dry fairly soft after wetting. (Smoked and unsmoked "Indian-tan" can be softened by kneading). The "Indian-tan" process is not patented, so make your own if you have the hides, space, and ambition.

Proving that traditional dress doesn't have to be fancy, with beads and feathers, here's Charles Seymore and his Salish-Flathead family, photographed in front of their tipi home in the Montana Rockies sometime around 1900. There are six children—his wife is behind his right shoulder—and like their dad, they all have on cotton shirts, wool leggings, breechcloths, buckskin moccasins, and braided hair, with the girls in calico dresses like their mom. Note that this was the common everyday style of traditional dress for the People of many tribes back in the wilderness days. Beadwork, feather headdresses, and bells were enjoyed on special occasions but would have been awkward for the ruggedness of daily tipi life.

Moccasins

On the following pages are outlines for several styles of moccasins—though many more existed, of course. Most tribes used certain traditional characteristics by which their moccasins could be told from those of similar styles used by other tribes. The two-piece moccasin style of the Plains, for instance, was worn by the People of many tribes. Some wore theirs without much decoration, while others liked to cover them partly or fully with lazy-stitch beadwork and still others decorated theirs with appliqué beadwork. Everyday moccasins were often plain.

The beaded designs, of course, differed among the tribes. The Cheyenne and Sioux preferred white backgrounds for their beadwork and often used complex geometric designs. The Blackfoot People preferred blue backgrounds and geometric designs made up of little squares and rectangles. On partially decorated moccasins they often sewed down a piece of colored cloth of a basic design and edged it with beads. Along with the Flatheads and other western neighbors, the Blackfoot also decorated their moccasins with beautiful flowers in appliqué beadwork.

The two-piece moccasin style has practically replaced the old one-piece style among the Blackfoot in more recent years. Their neighbors to the west, however, still use the one-piece style today. They invariably sew on ankle flaps to give their moccasins high tops for warmth, security, and protection against brush and snow.

Southern Plains moccasins were often cut quite low, but the People liked to add long fringes to the seams and cuffs. Women's moccasins in this area often had a top piece added on that reached almost to the knee. These top pieces were either buttoned up the sides or held up by a thong around the top. The tops were sometimes cut into fringes, which hung back down to the feet or just above them.

Moccasins worn by the desert People of the Southwest generally had separate soles made from thick hide and curved upwards around the edges. Sharp rocks and hot sands lined their trails and influenced their moccasin designs.

Tough, pliable leather is necessary for moccasins that are to be worn daily over trails. For soft-soled and one-piece styles, thick moosehide is best. For the bottoms of hard-soled styles, buffalo or steer rawhide is thickest and best. For winter wear use buffalo hide with the fur turned in. The one -piece style is best for this—well greased or covered with water repellent. Sinew is excellent for sewing up your moccasins—it is very tough and adds to the appearance. People in the old days always carried an awl and some sinew in a small pouch for moccasin and clothing repairs. When travelling away from home, one or more extra pairs of moccasins were carried in the pack or hung from the belt. It was common to find discarded moccasins next to the campfire remains of a passing hunting or war party. Others were thus able to tell what tribe the campers belonged to.

One-Piece Rocky Mountain Style

This is really a simple style of moccasin to make—even for one who has never sewn anything before. It is also one of the most handsome and comfortable styles to wear.

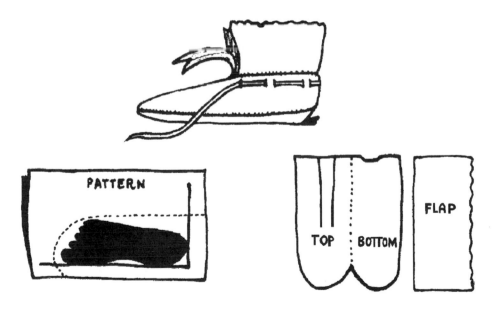

Make a paper pattern first, as shown, allowing the extra widths to make up for foot height. Use the pattern to make your leather pieces—be sure to reverse for left and right. Sew the pieces inside out and begin on

19

the short sewing side. When nearing the end of a long side, slip the piece on your foot, bring the two sides together up the heel, and mark the line of your heel on each side. Cut the ends slightly larger than marked, then sew from the top down to the cut-out rounded piece. Turn the moccasin right side out and stitch down the rounded piece to look neat. Trim the tongue and sew on an ankle flap to reach the desired height. Cut laces long enough to wrap around the ankle flap several times, and your new moccasins should fit securely.

Across the Northern Plains, through the Rocky Mountains, and westward nearly to the Pacific Coast, this woman's appearance was considered traditional in the late 1800s and early 1900s. She has on one-piece buckskin moccasins with high tops decorated by beadwork, a satin type of cloth dress, beaded belt, necklace and choker of shell disks, and a plaid shawl. Her thick hair is in two braids, tied at the bottom with strips of cloth. The purse, woven of corn husks, was made by several Plateau tribes, which may indicate her origin.

North Woods Style

This style of moccasin is still common today among the People of the widespread Cree and Chippewa tribes, many of whom continue to live by hunting and trapping in the remote northern woods. The making of this moccasin style requires patience and skill. The puckered toe section must be gathered properly to result in with an even foot covering.

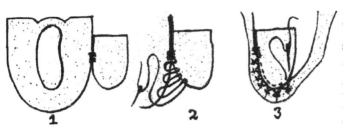

The first illustration of this style shows the shapes of the top and bottom pieces, with the foot outline drawn in. The large piece should be about two inches bigger than the outline of your foot, except in back. The smaller piece, called the "vamp," should measure about 3 by 5 inches for a man's moccasin. Part of this piece will form the tongue, so cut it longer than needed, and trim it after sewing.

Begin by stitching the two pieces together at the point where the curve begins, as in Figure 1. Figure 2 shows how the

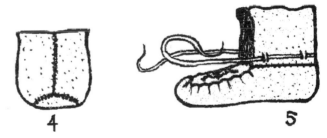

gathering is done—by taking stitches twice as large on the big piece as on the vamp. After the vamp is sewn on, insert a piece of wood or stone under the gathered ridges inside of the moccasin, and pound the ridges down flat on the outside with a hammer. Slip the moccasin over your foot (either one—this style has no left or right), and hold the sides up so that you can mark the heel line. Trim the surplus off the heel from the top down to the cut-out rounded piece. Stitch it on neatly to look like Figure 4. Add laces long enough to wrap around your ankles several times, and your moccasins should look like Figure 5. The vamps are often fully-beaded with the floral patterns used by the North Woods People. This should be done before sewing.

Southern Swamp Style

Variations of this moccasin style are worn by the People in the forests and swamps of the deep South—tribes such as the Seminole, Cherokee, and Muskogee.

Begin by cutting two rectangular pieces of leather like in Figure 1, each measuring about 12 by 20 inches. Cut the lacing strips from the pieces you trim off the corners of the pattern, as shown.

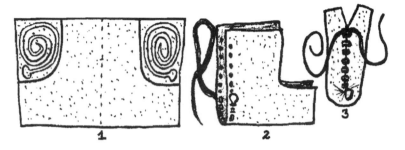

Punch holes along the longest straight section and run one lace in and out of the holes about one inch upon either side from the bottom, as in Figure 2. Pulling this lace tight should give you the puckered heel seen in Figure 3. Lace up the rest of the back of the moccasin round and round, as shown, and tie a knot at the end. Put a long thong through the top pair of holes to serve as ankle tie strings. Figure 4 shows the open front of the moccasin, with the laced-up heel showing in back. Insert a lace through the leather at the bottom front of the moccasin, and lace it up as in Figure 5. Pulling the laces tight will pucker up the toe and bring together the top of the moccasin as in Figure 6. Figure 7 shows the completed moccasin. By changing the pattern, the ankle flaps can be cut so that they are taller or so that they can be wrapped around the ankles.

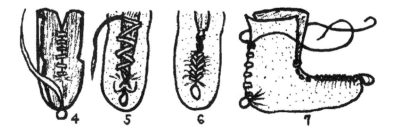

Top-Seam Style

This style of moccasin has the main seam running up the front center of the moccasin, beginning at the toes. The Kutenai variation is cut so that the two sides will fit perfectly together up to the vamp, which also serves as a tongue. The back and flaps are completed in the usual way. Of the other variations here illustrated, the one from the Shasta tribe of northern California is cut at an angle so that there will be a left and right to each pair. This requires careful gathering. With these top-seam styles, you may have to tear out your stitches several times before you end up with the proper fit and appearance. The other top-seam style was used in the East by the Ojibwa, Iroquois, and Shawnee.

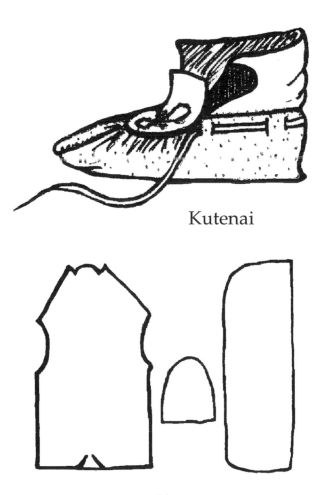

Kutenai

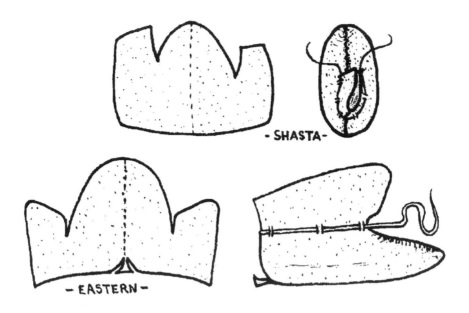

- SHASTA -

- EASTERN -

Pueblo Wrap-Around

This style of moccasin is commonly worn by the Zuni People but is popular in other Pueblos as well. The point marked A1 on the upper is sewn to the sole at the point marked "A." When the upper has been sewn all the way around the point marked, A2 is sewn down and cut off to slightly overlap A1. The piece B is then attached as a flap, with a buttonhole cut into it. The toe and heel of the sole is puckered, and a silver button holds the flap shut.

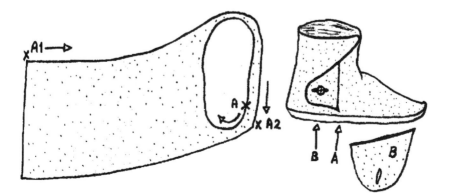

Southwest High Top

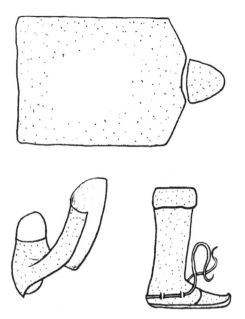

This style of moccasin is used by the People who live in the Pueblos of the Southwest. It has rawhide (or thick hide) soles and white deerskin uppers. The high top is sewn on first, and the toe piece is joined to it. The stitches are made on the outside and the sole leather is gathered at the toes and heels.

Plains Hard-Soled Style

This has always been one of the most popular moccasin styles. It is today's basic powwow style and was worn on the Plains in the past by the Sioux and their many neighbors. Sew inside out, beginning at A, first one along side to B, then the other. Sew up the back, add tongues and laces, then turn right side out.

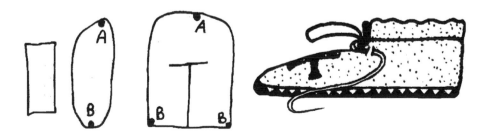

Here is a rugged pair of fully beaded Blackfoot moccasins, made of smoked deerhide with high ankle flaps. The simple flower and leaf pattern is done with beads of bright lavender and gold, backed by a solid covering of pale green beads in a firm appliqué stitch. Footwear like this was worn by both men and women among several tribes in the Northern Rockies and the Plains.

Picture courtesy Museum of the Plains Indian

Fur Robes and Wool Blankets

The fur robe was, in the Old Days, the most important item of dress—one of the most important single material items used by the Native People. With their robes, the People felt as secure as snails with their shells—they could curl tip under any bush and go to sleep in a warm bed. Or they could travel in any kind of weather and cover or uncover themselves as needed. If you have ever sat around an outdoor campfire wrapped up in a fine blanket, then you have some idea of the pleasure of robe-wearing.

The best fur robe in the old days was, of course, from the buffalo. Ideally, it was from a two-year-old cow. Many tribes who lived far from buffalo country sent good hunters on long journeys to bring back hides or else traded eagerly for them with tribes who had an extra supply. For years, any material thing among these People could be given a buffalo robe value—for, along with the horse, this was the standard item of exchange.

Buffalo robes can still be bought and are well worth their cost. Native tanners and reservation pawn shops sometimes sell tanned robes for as little as $50. Taxidermists and fur suppliers will ask closer to $200 for a new robe. Salted, untanned buffalo can at times be bought cheaply from private and government buffalo ranches and reserves, and from a few trading posts.

When worn, buffalo robes were generally wrapped the long way around the wearer's body. Among some tribes it was the custom to wear the head of the robe on the outside and facing to the left; among others it was a matter of preference. Robes with the fur left on (which were most common) were worn hair in or out, depending on the weather. Summer robes of buffalo and elk were worn without the hair. Some People cut the head and tail pieces off their robes for convenience, while others used only a part of the hide for their robes. Among some tribes it was the custom to

Rare photo of a rabbit skin robe worn by a young Cree woman in the manner of her ancestors far back in time. The People learned to use whatever skins and furs were available in their territory, including rabbit, buffalo, and everything in between.

Shawls and blankets were still part of everyday wear for these Salish-Flathead People in the 1880s, when they were photographed while visiting a general store in Missoula, Montana. Looking carefully you'll see three popular ways of wearing blankets. Mrs. Finlay, at left, has her shawl around her waist and over the left shoulder, leaving the right arm free. Her husband was Sam Finlay, the handsome fellow in the white shirt standing behind her, his braids wrapped with otter fur. Next to him is their friend, identified only as "Alex," holding his hat and wearing his loose hair tied in two bunches. Wearing short braids and funky white hat next to Alex, is "Joseph," whose blanket is wrapped tightly around the waist and reaches down nearly to his ankles. The next two fellows are not identified, but the nearest of them has his whole body covered by an early trade blanket with vivid designs. Missing from this photo is a fourth common blanket style, one used especially at night or in bad weather, where the whole body is wrapped and the head is also covered, leaving just a small opening around the face.

skin the hide of a buffalo in two long halves, tan it, and then sew the halves back together.

Robes were often decorated. The simpler styles involved painting the robe a solid color or covering it with black lines, Medicine designs, or pictographs of personal exploits. A more time-consuming method of decoration involved making a long, belt-like strip of quill or beadwork—as much as a foot wide and eight feet long—which was sewn down the center of the robe the long way. Usually four immense rosettes were spaced through this long strip, and quill work or buckskin thongs dangled from the center of these. Perhaps the most spectacular robe decorations were those which usually identified the chiefs and leading men; the skin sides of their robes were often nearly covered by yellow, orange, and red geometric designs, done in quill work, which combined to form gigantic sunbursts.

Rabbit skin blankets were popular among People who could not easily obtain buffalo robes. The whole skins sewn together do not make a very strong or neat blanket. Rather, the People cut the raw pelts into long strips about two inches wide, which they sewed end to end and rolled into a ball. After a period of days or months, when the ball appeared to be large enough, a wood frame loom was made—slightly larger than the desired blanket. The ball was unrolled and part of the long strip was wound upon the frame to form the warp. The remainder of the strip became the woof and was woven in and out of the warp. A light, fluffy, coarsely woven blanket was the result. Sometimes the fur strips were twisted as they were being rolled up and dried this way for the blanket.

Other light robes were made by the People from such furs as bear, which required two hides; wolf, which required four hides; and coyote, which sometimes required eight. These were trimmed to match and sewn with the fur sides together, using an overhand stitch. Worn fur out, the seams appeared as even ridges that contrasted the different skins.

Red squirrel skin robes were sometimes popular, according to one Sioux craftsman, who said: "Old women also tanned the hides, and when they got enough together, they made little robes on which to sit to smoke their pipes."

Blankets became very popular after their introduction by traders, because they are lighter and less bulky than robes. Blue wool blankets with white, undyed edges were most common among the central and southern tribes. In the north the Point blankets from the Hudson's Bay Company were and are a favorite with all outdoor people. In the Northwest and Plateau areas, the many-colored Pendelton blankets and shawls have long been favorites and are today very commonly seen at powwows from Oregon to Oklahoma.

Robes and blankets were worn in a variety of ways, both for comfort and for particular style. For instance, young men generally wore theirs wrapped around the body so that the arms remained free, or else over their heads so that only their faces were showing (a common style when courting). Women generally wore theirs over both shoulders, or over their heads in colder weather. They often fastened a belt around the robe at the waist so that the blanket could be dropped to free the hands for working. Old men often left their right arms free and held the ends of their robes with their left hands from underneath.

For sleeping, the robe or blanket is spread open on the ground. The sleeper then lays on one end, folds the blanket over him, and tucks the other end beneath himself. The bottom of this bed roll is then folded up underneath the legs.

Old-Time Overcoats

A handmade overcoat is one of the easiest and most functional old-time dress items that you might make. Two basic styles exist: the blanket capote and the northern parka. Both have sleeves and hoods and are very practical for life in the outdoors. Capotes are generally made from warm blankets, while parkas are generally made from furs. However, any material which you may have on hand, or wish to obtain, can be used. The main consideration is your intended use of the coat.

Northern Parka

The parka is the simpler to make of the two overcoats. Make a paper pattern as illustrated—allow yourself a loose fit for heavy clothing underneath—then cut your material accordingly.

Begin by sewing the front and back together at the shoulders (A). Next, sew up the sides, beginning at the bottom and up to the sleeve holes (B). Attach the sleeve pieces, beginning at A, and then sew these from where they are attached up to the cuffs. Stitch the hood together from the front (C) on up, and the parka will be completed.

Parkas are often made in contrast—soft, warm material worn inside; tough, waterproof material covering the outside.

NORTHERN PARKA

C C

HOOD

A

BACK

B

Blanket Capote

French trappers in the Canadian woods gave this fine coat its name, and all those who have worn one understand its winter fame. It is easy to make and enjoyable to wear; all you need is a blanket and a little time.

More capotes have been made with the striped Hudson's Bay Point blankets than any other. The white ones with colored stripes were especially popular, although the red ones with black stripes were also often used. Any large wool blanket will make a nice warm capote, however.

Cut up your blanket according to the drawing. To avoid much unravelling, tear your material whenever the line for cutting falls along the "straight." Notice that the body of the capote (back and fronts) is all one piece—all you need to sew is the shoulders. (The extra lengths that are shown folded back on the sleeves, neck, and front of the hood are for fringes, and may be left out.) Next, sew up the back of the hood, and attach it to the body at the neck and lapels. Hoods generally had tassels hanging from them, one sewn to each of the three sides at the tip. Your capote is now ready to wear. Tie strings may be sewn on or a belt or sash used to hold the capote closed.

Capote is a French term describing long coats made from trade blankets, commonly worn by early trappers and traders, adopted from them as a popular style by the men of several Northern Plains tribes, especially the Blackfeet. Most capotes were made from blankets decorated with colored stripes, such as those offered by the Hudson's Bay Company. These blankets were cut so that the stripes went around the sleeves and main body as seen in this photo, taken at a Blackfoot camp around 1900. The man is holding his tack-decorated knife sheath, attached to a belt that would normally be worn around the waist over the capote, keeping it closed in place of buttons.

For a pleasing appearance, bind all exposed edges with colored cloth or ribbon, as shown in the drawing. Use the same material to cover the shoulder and sleeve seams.

These last two bindings were sometimes fully or partially covered with beadwork. Large rosettes were sometimes added to the front of the hood, while beads and sequins were often tacked on top of or parallel with the bindings. Capotes can also be made of moose hide or buffalo fur.

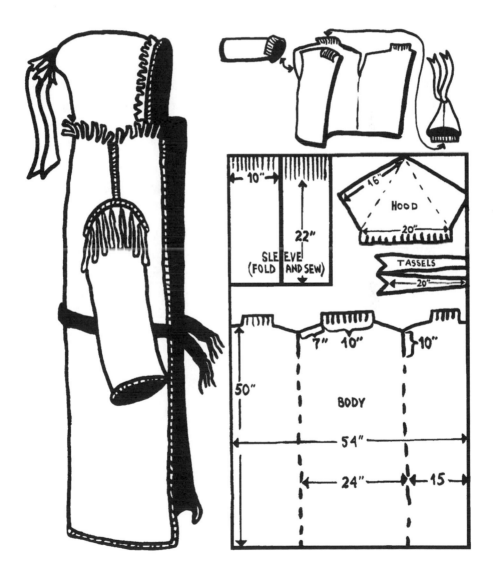

Mittens and Socks

Footwear in the winter time and during cold rains was no easy matter in the Old Days. One old Comanche woman once told an anthropologist who wondered about the Native secret for winter warmth: "Some folks were just awfully cold all winter."

For basic foot warmth, tall winter moccasins were made of buffalo hide with the fur turned in. Extra buffalo fur or other warm skins were wrapped around the feet for more protection, and pieces of dried and shaped rawhide were tied over the outside to keep out moisture. Bear or other animal fat was often melted and used to coat moccasins to keep out water. Unfortunately, moisture always got in, leather slipped on snow and ice, and pausing in cold weather sometimes meant frozen lumps at the ends of the legs.

Socks were often cut and sewn in the form of foot-sized pouches. These were folded around the ankles and held up by the wrapped tops of the moccasins.

Gloves were apparently not made in the Old Days, but mittens were generally worn over the hands in cold weather. Mittens keep the hands warmer than gloves by allowing the fingers more movement. Mittens are also easy to remove in a hurry—they were generally attached to each other by a thong worn over the shoulder, so that they could be allowed to fall

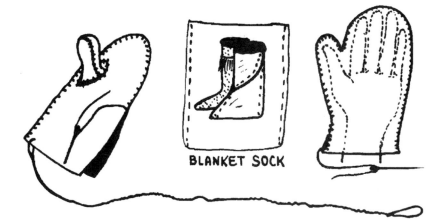

BLANKET SOCK

from the hands. Two basic styles were made, one with the thumb and hand cut as one piece, the other with a separate thumb piece sewn over an opening for the thumb. Both kinds were made from single pieces folded over and sewn up or two pieces sewn all the way around.

Proud men of the Northern Plains and Rockies wore fancy gauntlets like these just to improve their appearance, even though they were of no practical use for daily living. The multicolored beadwork is light blue, royal blue, red, yellow, and green. It was done in a fine appliqué stitch using two threads, making it so flat and firm that it could last for several generations. Blackfoot geometric beadwork is notable for its use of many small designs to create larger ones, such as the rhomboid isosceles in the middle here. Green pony beads are strung on the outer fringes.

Picture courtesy Museum of the Plains Indian

This young dancer of the Spokane tribe has on the traditional dress of his eastern Washington People from around 1900. Panel leggings and a long, dark shirt serve as background for his fully beaded vest, armband, belt, and gauntlets. He also has a feather belt trailer decorated with various birds. The buffalo horn staff in his hand was just a dance decoration, but the feathers and fur trailer in the other hand seems to be a sacred object. He wears more furs as part of his shoulder bandoleer, as well.

Belts

Belts were very important articles to people who lived outdoors and whose clothing had no pockets. From belts hung their knives, awls, and handy pouches. Men used belts to hold up their leggings and breech-cloths—women used them to keep their dresses in place.

Belts were commonly made out of heavy leather or rawhide. Commercial harness leather has long been a favorite belt material and was used exclusively whenever it was available. Men's belts were generally no more than three inches wide, but women's belts of five and six inches were not unusual. The simple method of fastening a belt was to have a buckskin thong attached through two holes in one end, and then slipped through two matching holes in the other end and tied in front. Harness buckles and uniform buckles were sometimes sewn on instead.

Beads, brass tacks, and metal conchos were the main items used to decorate belts. Small brass tacks (similar to those used on upholstery) were often pushed through the leather and the protruding points broken off. These were the popular "tack belts" of the Northern Plains. Tack belts were either solidly covered by even rows of tacks, or designs were made by using tacks or leaving certain areas untacked.

"Panel belts" were another popular type on the Northern Plains. These were decorated by sections, or panels, of lazy-stitch beadwork (often with rows so long between stitches that they hung loosely over each other). This beadwork was alternated with undecorated sections or with sections of brass tacks.

Fully beaded belts were used most everywhere. Lazy-stitch and appliqué beadwork was done on the belt itself, which was usually made of stiff leather or soft leather with heavy backing. Beaded belts made on a loom were generally sewn to a stiff backing.

Belts covered by trade metal or silver conchos (from less than one to several inches in diameter) were most popular on the Central and Southern Plains. The conchos were usually attached by a long thong running behind the belt. Women's concho belts often had a matching piece hanging down one side and sometimes ending with an ornate silver tip.

Traditional dress of the Pueblo People in the Southwest looks distinct from all other tribes, as seen on this woman here at Santa Clara Pueblo in New Mexico during the 1890s. Her clothing is loose and partly wrapped around her. The shawl-like head covering was worn by both men and women to help protect against the hot sun and strong, sandy winds. A woven sash around the waist helps to hold her outfit together. High-topped moccasins of thick hide help protect against rocky, sandy ground, and cactus spines, plus snakes and insects. The beautiful pot on her head is typical for Pueblo People, each village having its own styles that continue to be made today. The ladder on her adobe-walled and log-beamed house leads to an upper story. In the past there were no doors on the lower floors, so the ladder could be drawn up in case of attack by enemies

In the Southwest and Northeast very fine hand-woven sashes were often used instead of belts. The sashes of the Hopi (which are woven by the men) have become standard items for the ceremonial wear of many Southwest tribes. Sashes are often quite wide and so long that they have to be wrapped several times around the waist. Long fringe often hangs from the ends. In the North a popular belt was the "Hudson's Bay Assumption Sash," which is basically red with many colors interwoven. It was worn by Natives and trappers alike.

Armbands and anklets were, and are, usually worn with dance outfits, but were not often worn with everyday dress. Armbands were decorated with quill or beadwork, or made from strips of fur (often the foot sections with claws or hooves still attached). Metal bands were cut from brass sheets and tin cans. Strips of angora or buffalo fur were worn over the feet, tied beneath sleigh bells that were fastened to leather straps.

Beading

Beadwork decoration is a fine method for emphasizing pride in the design and workmanship of one's belongings. Beads vary in size from a pin head to a pigeon egg, some rare types being even larger. After they became readily available from traders, the Native Americans used beads in countless different ways. With the tiny "seed" beads, they developed a complex art form that was used to decorate clothing, tools, and even riding equipment. This art form was based on the ancient method of decorating by sewing down dyed and flattened porcupine quills.

Four methods of beadwork are commonly used. The easiest of these is done on a loom. A loom is easily made of wood, and should be about three inches wide and six inches longer than your planned beadwork. The tops of the upright pieces need grooves spaced ⅛ inch apart to hold the warp threads. Use heavy thread for the warp, and weave it back and forth across the loom and around the screws at each end as shown in the drawing. Wax all thread with beeswax to keep it from slipping.

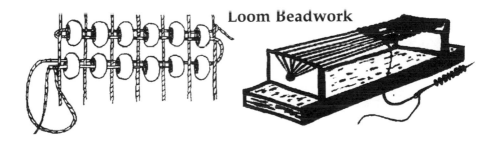

Loom Beadwork

Headbands, belts, and hat bands are generally made on a loom. Plan the design on paper, and leave two warp threads on each side, for strength. Beads are strung on the weave thread, spaced across the warp threads, and pushed down to be passed through again by the weave thread below the warp. Begin in the middle and work towards the ends. Weave back and forth a few times to finish, and knot the warp threads together. Attach the completed bead strip to a leather backing by sewing down the double-warp edges with strong thread.

More creative beadwork can by made with the "lazy-stitch" method. Finished pieces done this way are distinctive for their ridged rows of somewhat loose beads. This produced an appearance that was especially popular among the People of the Plains. It was done by sewing several beads at a time directly to leather, these being attached only at the ends of rows.

Lazy-stitch beadwork is generally applied directly to the item to be decorated. A knot is tied at the end of a waxed thread and hidden on the reverse side of the beadwork. From two to more than ten beads are strung at a time and sewn down in the parallel rows. The needle does not go entirely through the material but catches only the outer edge of it. Figure A is a top view of the beads before being pulled tight. Figure B is a side view.

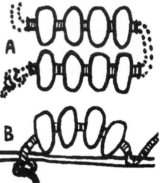

The third style of beadwork is known as the "appliqué stitch." Two threads are used, and every second or third bead is sewn down. This method produces the most perfect beadwork on leather. It is ideal for floral and pictorial designs. It was very popular among the People of the Rocky Mountain country, as well as the Woodlands People in the East.

The end of one thread is knotted and attached to the material. A number of beads are strung on it and laid in place. The second thread is then sewn across the first one, a stitch being taken at every second or third bead. Between stitches the second thread passes under the beads, just below the surface if using leather. When beading on cloth, the material must be backed for support, and the thread must be pulled all the way through. Beads may be sewn down in straight lines or in curves, as fits the design. Completed appliqué beadwork presents such a smooth, tight appearance that no threads are visible.

Circular pieces of beadwork are known as rosettes. They are often used where only a small amount of beadwork is desired—on leather vests, purses, and fur caps, for instance. They may range in size from a dime to a dinner plate.

Rosettes are generally made on backed felt or buckskin. Begin by drawing a circle on the material, and then draw in the design. Don't cut the circle out until you have done the beadwork. Knot the waxed thread and sew down the center bead. Sew down the first row two beads at a time. Go back through the second bead again each time. After the first row, sew down four beads at a time, and go back through the last two. At the end of each row, run the thread through all the beads again if they need to be evened up.

A man of the Sarcee tribe is seen in this 1890s photo wearing an old-time looking shirt with its beaded strips and leather fringes. The main part is actually wool, styled as though it were buckskin. A two-strand bead choker and a brass chain bandoleer are his simple jewelry, with a fur strip tied to one of his scanty braids, probably for spiritual reasons. A good part of his hair is cut short on top, in a popular style.

This Sioux-style buckskin dress was probably the finest clothing belonging to its owner back in the late 1800s, when tiny seed beads were still fairly new and valuable. The interesting stars and roses across the front are bordered by beaded lines with geometric patterns, matched along the bottom of the dress as well. The beadwork is done in lazy-stitch style, with rows of sequins sewn along the edges.

Photograph courtesy of Museum of the Plains Indian

Here's a buckskin dress that would stand out at any gathering with its combination of brightly colored beadwork and a variety of other decoration. The flowered frontispiece is fully beaded in appliqué stitches and surrounded by rows of drilled cowrie shells that have long been popular items of trade. Below the frontispiece hang long strands of glass basket beads in at least two colors. Two-holed sequins are sewn in a row along the neck, and below them is a row of heart-shaped shells, plus small tassels of beads.

Photograph courtesy Museum of the Plains Indian

Women's Clothing

The simplest style of women's clothing was that seen among tribes in warm weather regions. Skirts of tule, woven grass, and shredded bark were worn by women along both sea coasts. Aprons and skirts of animal furs were also common. Blankets and robes of various styles were worn by such women when the weather got cold, or at nighttime.

The simple styles mentioned above can be assembled using your own imagination. We will limit this discussion to the more complex dress items—leather and cloth dresses and leggings—as they were made and worn from the deserts of the Southwest to the woods of the Northeast.

The most common style of leather dress of the Old Days was made like a slip, with shoulder straps and separate sleeves tied around the neck and sometimes under the arms, as illustrated. It was seen among numerous tribes.

Another old style of dress (though apparently more recent than the one just described) was made from two deer skins. The three drawings show the steps in making this dress. The skins are laid together; the dotted line marks the eventual shoulder line. The bottom of the dress is trimmed to suit the wearer's taste (or the tribal style) and also the size. Commonly, the bottom of the dress was arranged so that all or part of the legs on the skins were left hanging at each side, and sometimes the tail was left to hang down in the front and back

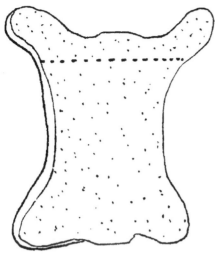

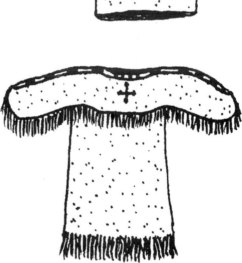

centers. The two pieces are
sewn together with sinew or
thread or laced with leather
strips, with an in-and-out stitch
along the dotted line. The sides
are sewn down with an overhand stitch. The tops of the
hides are folded down, front
and back, to form the yoke, as
shown. A neck opening is cut
and hemmed. The sleeves may
be sewn shut, laced together, or
just left hanging open.

Sometimes the hides were sewn so that their hinds formed the yoke,
and the deer tails were left to hang down the front. Sometimes they were
tailored so that fringes could be cut right into the dress itself; at other
times strips of leather were sewn on separately and fringed, often up
along the side seam.

James A. Teit, who was married to a woman of the Salish People,
described their styles of dresses:

"Women's dresses were made of two whole Deerskins or small
Elk skins sewed face to face heads down, the sides were sewed

An elderly Yakima woman in her finest dress of buckskin, its cape fully decorated with pony beads.

Photo by L.V. McWhorter
Yakima, Washington, 1912

up to near the armpits. At the upper ends of the skins the edges were folded over and sewed down to the body of the garment. There were no sleeves, the extensions of the shoulders consisting of the hind legs of the skins falling over the arms almost to the wrists. The side seams and all the outer edges were fringed. Generally the tail-pieces were cut off and the bottom of the dress trimmed so that it was longer at the sides. Usually one or two rows of inserted thongs descended from the dress near the bottom. In later days some cloth dresses, generally red and blue, were used instead of skin. They were cut and ornamented in much the same way as the skin dresses."

Dress Decorations

Tribal styles of dress decorations were generally similar to the decorations on men's shirts and leggings. Tribes of the Southwest and Southern Plains liked to paint their leather clothing in solid colors, sometimes with contrasting lines along the edges. They had a strong liking for long, thin fringes hanging in profusion. Items of silver, especially buttons and conchos, were common on their dresses, leggings, and moccasins. Heavy beadwork on yokes was rare, but narrow lines of beadwork were often used to decorate seams and edges.

Yokes fully covered with bead and quill work were most common among the Sioux People and their neighbors. These women certainly looked striking with their long braids falling over an immense section of beadwork that was covered with geometric designs and sometimes reached the waist. Some women who could afford vast quantities of dentalium shells covered their yokes with row upon row of these fine items. Elk teeth, however, were the most prized of all dress decorations among many tribes in addition to the Sioux. Those who could not afford solid rows of teeth (and few could) were often content to space the rows far apart or to add some teeth to the bottom of a row of beadwork. Cowrie shells gave a similar effect for much less expense and were particularly popular on the heavy wool replacements of skin dresses. By that time restricted hunting had made teeth even more valuable. The Sioux even carved elk teeth replicas from bone.

50

Close-up on an old wool cape made for a Blackfoot girl in the latter 1800s. Rows of small seed beads vary by color, with cowrie shells attached by bead-strung threads to hang underneath. The wool material is lined with lighter cloth and edged at the neck and arms. This cape would be worn over an ordinary dress of cloth or leather.

Photograph courtesy Museum of the Plains Indian

Old-time Blackfoot dresses were commonly decorated with a band of beadwork across the front that curved downward toward the center. Another beaded band often covered the shoulders, and small beaded symbols were applied on other parts of the dresses. A downward-pointing triangle, a traditional symbol of fertility, was generally beaded on the lower front of the dress. A narrow beaded band usually edged the bottom of the dress, while thongs and fringes often hung in profusion. Blackfoot women preferred beads larger than seed beads for their dresses. They used both pony beads and glass tube beads on the capes. Time saved made up for beauty lost. Large beads were also strung on the long thongs, while thimbles and drilled coins were attached to their ends and deer hooves and cowrie shells were tied into the fringes.

Cloth dresses were decorated in a variety of ways, in addition to, or instead of, beadwork. Cowrie shells were popular, and ribbon edging was almost always applied around the bottom. Heavy wool dresses were usually edged with one or more rows of narrow ribbons and sometimes with wide ribbons at the bottom. Brass sequins, shoe buttons, and similar items were often sewn down next to the narrow ribbon edging. Designs such as crosses and circles were also made with them. Dresses made of light cloth usually had one or two wide ribbons sewn on at the bottom. Chippewa women commonly attached many rows of tin cone jingles to their cloth dresses.

Women of Prairie tribes, such as the Osage and Sac and Fox, developed elaborate cloth skirts and dresses by using ribbon decoration. Ribbons (and ribbon-like strips of cloth) were sewn down in vertical and horizontal rows of varying widths. Contrasting ribbon was then folded in half and cut, like children's paper cutouts, into floral and geometrical designs. The contrasting ribbons with the design holes cut in them were then sewn over the basic ribbons, so that the basic ribbons could be seen through the design holes. The cut out pieces of contrasting ribbon could also be sewn onto the basic ribbons. Much careful sewing and hemming is required to give this style the beauty that its design highlights.

Other common articles of women's clothing included belts, moccasins, headgear, and necklaces, which are all described elsewhere. Little pouches for toilet and sewing articles, as well as a slender case for an awl, were often carried from a belt or tied elsewhere on the dress. Bracelets of small beads and metal, as well as rings of metal and silver, were much desired. Fringed shawls have been very popular shoulder coverings since they have been available.

A young woman of the Plateau region wears a fully beaded cape, and leggings and moccasins to match, with her fringed buckskin dress and her long breastplate of hairpipes and glass beads. This would be considered a traditional outfit among the women of many western tribes, each of whom made their own changes and variations through the passing generations.

Jesse Spotted Eagle and his wife illustrate the style of dress worn by their Nez Perce People in the late 1800s. She wears a nicely patterned cloth dress which is complimented by her fringed shawl. A wool shawl serves as his breechcloth, worn nearly to the ground. He also wears wool leggings, a cloth shirt, a loop necklace, and a single eagle feather at the back of his loose hair. The dancing stick in his hand probably had spiritual meanings, with a red fox skin at one end and a varied bunch of feathers at the other. The photograph was taken in an Idaho studio.

Jicarilla Apache Deerskin Dress

Of the two basic styles used in the making of most buckskin dresses, Teit describes one, and this Apache dress illustrates the other. It is basically a dress made of two hides, sewn up the sides and across the top, except for a neck opening and the openings of the short sleeves. Instead of folding over the top of the dress, however, a separate yoke is added. In this case, the yoke falls down a short distance, front and back, and is generally sparsely decorated. Similar yokes were made by Sioux women. Theirs came down much lower, were usually cut straight across at the bottom, and were often fully covered with beadwork of much weight.

The fringes were cut from separate pieces of leather that were sewn along the inside edges and between the side hems. Pieces of leather were sometimes added between the side seams to make the skirts fuller.

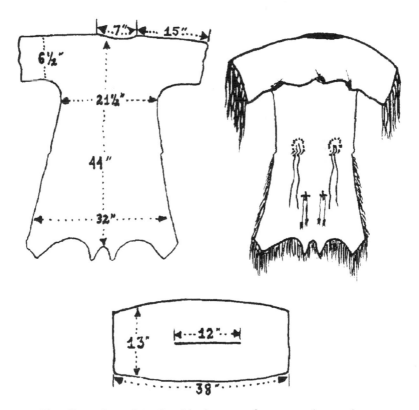

The dimensions given for this dress are for proportions only.

Three Jicarilla Apache women are seen outside their tipi near Dulce, New Mexico, around 1910. They are wearing cloth adaptations of their traditional dress styles. The woman on the left is working on an Apache-style basket, the one in the middle is beading on a long wooden loom, and the old lady at the right is preparing clay for another pot like the one on the ground next to her. All three of the women are wearing blankets, two around the waist and one over her shoulders.

Cloth Dresses

Women, more than men, must have been greatly pleased with the coming of cloth. The majority of full dress-wearing tribes adopted a physical modesty that must have made the heavy skin dresses of the women a sheer burden when travelling on hot days, cooking in crowded lodges, or gathering wood, water, berries, and stray children from near and far.

For warmth and style, heavy wool "trade cloth" was the most popular for dresses. These were generally made like the old skin dresses. Often, in

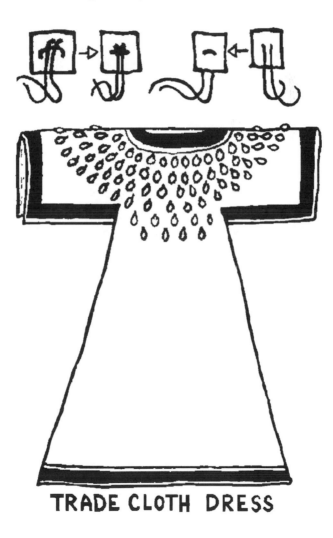

TRADE CLOTH DRESS

This traditional Cheyenne girl is wearing her best outfit for a visit to town, or maybe to have her picture taken on the front porch of the government agent's house. Her dress is of dark wool trade cloth with the colored selvage edge left on as trim for the sleeves and bottom, along with rows of sequins and small beaded crosses. The top half of her dress is decorated with yellow cowrie shells. She also wears a long hairpipe and bead breastplate, plus a belt and long drop of leather covered with silver conches. She carries a bead-decorated cradleboard that may have held a newborn sibling or a nearly life-sized doll.

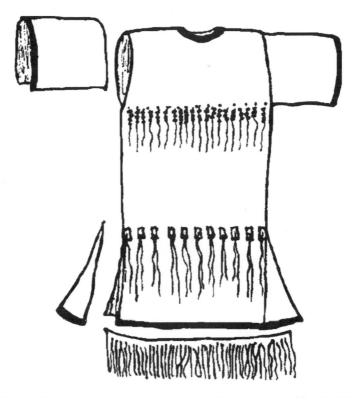

fact, buckskin fringes were sewn on at the bottoms, and buckskin thongs were suspended in rows across the dresses, sometimes anchored to small pieces of colored cloth. Two methods of attaching these thongs are illustrated. Many times the beaded or quilled yokes from worn-out skin dresses were repaired and worn over plain cloth dresses.

The large, and sometimes annoying, sleeves of many old skin dresses were often modified on cloth dresses. Sometimes the cloth sleeves were just made slimmer; other times they had cuffs that buttoned. With the latter, a loose blouse was often worn which had big, open-ended and elbow-length sleeves. At other times the dress had flaring sleeves, and a blouse with cuffs was worn underneath. The combination of blouse and dress gave more warmth and the appearance was pleasing—especially when contrasting calico materials were used. Aprons were sometimes worn in the form of a second skirt—made of yet another contrasting pattern of calico material. This style became the everyday dress for numerous women after the start of the reservation period, and variations of it may still be commonly seen today.

Trade cloth dresses of the style worn by this Kutenai woman became popular through-out the Northern Plains and Rockies in the later 1800s and continue to be worn at powwows and special events today. The upper part of this dress is covered with bead-ed flowers, then edged with ribbons. A nice contrast is made by the light-colored blouse that she wears underneath. Her necklace is made up of white glass tube beads with rows of smaller pony beads as spacers, similar to her choker. Although it does reach her waist, the necklace is not nearly as long as it seems, since this lower section is actually the bead-decorated drop of her wide belt, which barely shows under her right arm. She holds a decorated bag woven from corn husks and wears a narrow beaded strip as a headband. Note the pointed toes of her buckskin moccasins, a distinctive Kutenai style. Their high tops are covered by a pair of woolen leggings decorated with beaded edges and a row of brass buttons.

L. G. Bigelow Photo—Ronan, Montana

Apache Skin Poncho

Leather ponchos were commonly worn by women of many tribes over bare skin in the long ago. More recently they were worn over leather and cloth dresses for added warmth and appearance. The styles were basically the same, while the decorations can easily be imagined. The Apache liked very long fringe on theirs and often painted them a solid color. In cold areas, these ponchos were sometimes made of buffalo or other fur with the hair worn inside.

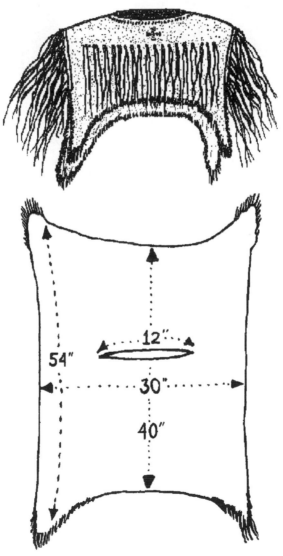

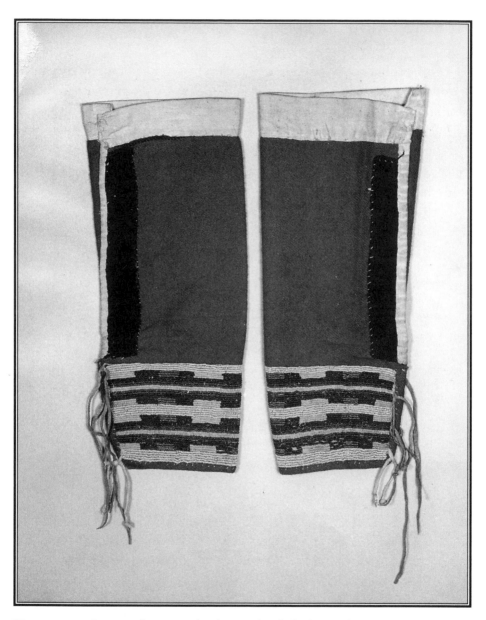

The women of many tribes wore leggings under their dresses for warmth and protection. This pair is from the Blackfeet and was made of wool trade cloth in the late 1800s. They are edged with cotton, with the bottom panel fully beaded in appliqué stitch. Leather laces and old shoe buttons usually close up the sides.

Photograph courtesy of Museum of the Plains Indian

Women's Leggings

There was generally little or no difference between the moccasins worn by the men and the women of the same tribe. In the Plains area, however, women wore snug-fitting leggings beneath their dresses which covered their legs from the ankles to somewhere around the knees, the height depending on tribal style. Everyday leggings were often simply two pieces of buckskin cut to wrap around the lower leg, wider at the top than bottom. Several thongs were used to tie the leggings together along the

outside of the legs. Long thongs were used to hold the tops up. When worn with high-top moccasins, the leggings were usually wrapped around the outside of the ankle flaps.

One style of legging was made to be worn inside the ankle flaps of high-top moccasins. In the drawings on the previous page this style is shown with shoe buttons along the side. These were sometimes used instead of tie strings whenever they could be obtained. A strip of colored cloth was sometimes sewn down one side over the buttonholes for decoration.

The most common decoration on leggings consisted of a panel of bead-work that usually covered the bottoms of the leggings. Women on the Southern Plains often made and decorated their leggings to match their moccasins. In the North the decoration generally contrasted with the moc-casins and usually consisted of designs done within narrow bands of beadwork. Sometimes the beadwork was solid; other times it merely high-lighted a background of colored cloth, such as dark green velvet.

Men's Clothing

A young Nez Perce warrior named Tom Gould. Shows the finest style of traditional dress among his people in the late 1800s. His buckskin shirt is decorated on the shoulders and sleeves with tanned weasel skins the same as his leggings, with a row of human hair locks across his chest. He also wears a split-horn headdress decorated with many weasels. Such clothing was only worn by men of distinction, mainly noted warriors and chiefs.

Men's Shirts

Buckskin shirts were not as common in the Old Days as has often been assumed. In fact, shirts were not made or worn by the men of many tribes until fairly late in the period of the old life. Those shirts that were worn long ago were generally in the style of ponchos, with loose sleeves attached. They were often left open along the sides and only fastened by a couple of thongs underneath the sleeves. The neck opening was usually a large slit that was tied shut with thongs at the shoulders.

A simple style of shirt was worn by men in the Northwest forests—and probably in other areas, as well. It consisted of a large deer hide that was folded in half, with a slit cut along the fold for a head opening. It was stitched or laced up the sides and arms (which were simply left as part of the hide when the sides were trimmed), or tied with thongs that also served as fringe.

Another simple shirt was made of two deerskins that were sewn together heads up. The heads and necks were trimmed off and the resulting gap allowed the wearer's head to pass through. The forelegs were fastened together in pairs to form the sleeves. The shirt was sometimes trimmed straight across the bottom, often fringed, and other times left complete, with the legs hanging far down on each side of the wearer.

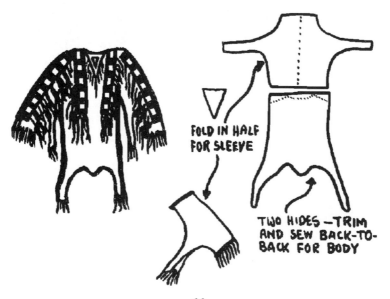

FOLD IN HALF FOR SLEEVE

TWO HIDES—TRIM AND SEW BACK-TO-BACK FOR BODY

Extra long fringes decorate the back of this man's buckskin shirt that was made by the noted Blackfeet craftworker, Julia-Wades-In-The-Water, in the early 1900s. The bead-work of red dots on a white background is quite unusual, but the triangular neck flap is of a common design. The shirt's short length and straight-cut bottom identifies it as being made after the old days. Glass basket beads are strung to the tops of the fringes. This shirt was made to fulfill a dream by the Blackfeet leader, Wades-In-The-Water.

Warm shirts for winter wear were made in a number of ways, generally from hides with the hair left on. A small buffalo robe, for instance, was commonly folded in half, an opening cut for the head, and the sides fastened together. Two coyote skins were sometimes worn over the front and back, with tails hanging down. Pieces of other skins were used to attach these two together at the shoulders and sides.

Shirt Decorations

Two basic methods of ornamenting shirts were used by most all shirt-wearing tribes and were found to some degree on most all leather shirts. One of these, of course, was fringe. Some Hopi shirts had only a few short fringes cut from the excess material that protrudes from their style of seams. Some Kutenai shirts had amazingly long fringes sewn into the seams at the sides, shoulders, and arms, as well as fringes cut into the neck

Tin-Tin-Meet-Sa, or Willowskin, eighty-year-old chief of the Umatilla tribe of Oregon. He is wearing a weasel-decorated buckskin shirt of the type that had sacred and ceremonial meaning among several tribes of the Northern Plains and the Western Plateau country. He wears his hair loose, a common style in the pre-reservation era, but limited mainly to old men by the time of this 1909 photo, taken by Rodman Wannamaker at the "Last Great Council of Chiefs" on the Crow Reservation in Montana. Said the old chief at that time:

> "My days have been spent for many suns along the great rivers and high mountains of Oregon. It has been many years ago that I was selected by our agent as the head man of my tribe. In those days I was a very active man, but since I have become so old, although they look upon me as the head man of the tribe, I must leave this work for others to do ...

> "This country (eastern Montana) all looks familiar to me because, in my younger days, I traveled all over these prairies fighting the Sioux Indians who had stolen horses from my tribe (and) to hunt the buffalo ... I can scarcely see, but my eyes could still find the old trails. The buffalo has gone, and I am soon going ... The record here made will not perish ... I have no hard feelings toward anyone ... and I am only worrying about my hay at home."

opening and across the shirt bottoms. These, no doubt, produced some memorable experiences when their wearers chased game or tried to escape from enemies in the dense brush of their country. The People of the Southern Plains, too, liked long fringe on their shirts and garments. They often cut their fringes very thin and numerous. Each fringe was moistened and then rolled with the palm of the hand across the lap, which left the fringes with a very pleasing spiralled appearance.

Along with fringe, the other basic shirt ornament was the triangular flap which hung down from the front and back of the neck. This flap helped to cover the often large neck openings, besides adding a pleasing dimension to the front of the shirt. The flaps were commonly fringed on the edges and covered with paint or painted designs, as well as quill and beadwork.

The famous Chief Geronimo shows the traditional fringed buckskin shirt of his Apache People, with a horned feather headdress that symbolized his leadership and a striped blanket around his waist. With the pistol, he must have been contemplating how he entered history as North America's last great fighting chief.

Buckskin shirts are often called war shirts, though among many tribes the shirts that were used in war were of a particular—and sacred—character, and seldom worn. Many shirts were, however, painted and decorated for war purposes, even if used at other times. The specific decorations were, of course, first seen in dreams. They included these methods:

Shirts painted a solid color

Shirts painted several colors, such as yellow top and sleeves and red bottom

Shirts covered with painted designs, such as large stripes all around, crosses, dots, etc.

Other Medicine figures

Shirts perforated all over with circles or other designs

Other war shirts were recognizable by certain tribal styles and by the knowledge that the wearer was a successful warrior. Sometimes the wearers of these shirts belonged to societies, and often they were offered large payments if they were willing to part with a shirt to some aspiring young man who felt that he would gain extra strength through its wearing.

Among the Sioux People, decorated shirts were worn only by leaders in the Old Days. The most important of these leaders belonged to a group called the Wicasas—The Shirt Wearers. They were the only ones to wear painted shirts. The Wicasas were chosen from among the bravest and most honorable men of the tribe and served as official executives—men above reproach. Their shirts were usually painted either blue and yellow or red and green. The colors of the paintings represented aspects of the Universe, while the fringes of hair locks represented the people of the tribe. The famous Sioux chief Crazy Horse was such a Shirt Wearer.

Other common shirt decorations were the stripes of quill and beadwork that were worn down the arms and over the shoulders. Blackfoot shirts often had a large beaded medallion in front of the chest, as well as fringes of white with black-tipped ermine skins. In later years the sacred hair-lock shirts became more generally used. The hair locks were sometimes enemy scalps, but more commonly were made from horse hair or hair donated by friends and relatives.

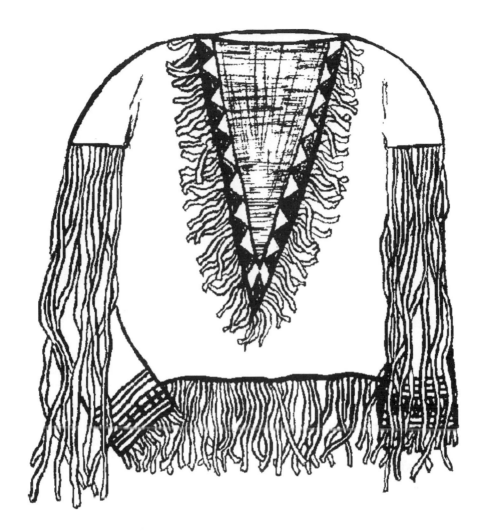

Taos Elk Skin Shirt

In the Old Days, the men of the Taos Pueblo in New Mexico often travelled north to the Plains country in order to hunt buffalo. Though they were members of the Southwest Pueblo culture—a life of farming and permanent villages—they saw many appealing aspects of the buffalo hunting tribes on the Plains, some of which they brought home and adopted themselves. This shirt is a typical example of a Taos-Plains article.

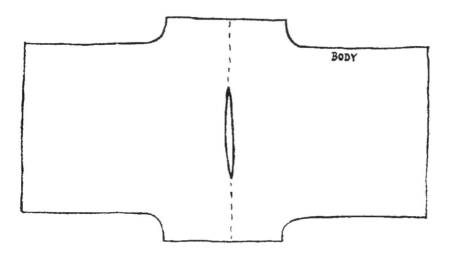

The shirt requires two deer hides or one large elk hide. The main section is one piece that is cut like a poncho, as seen in the drawing. The measurements given are only for proportion—yours will depend on your own size and desires.

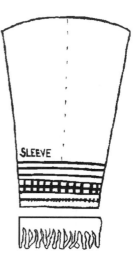

Begin by cutting a 10-or 12-inch slit for the head opening in the piece which you have cut to shape. Then lay the body and sleeve pieces on the floor, attaching them as shown, and sew them together. A long, rectangular piece of buckskin is sewn between each sleeve and the body. This is later fringed. These fringe pieces should hang lower than the bottoms of the sleeves. The sleeves and shirt sides may either be sewn shut (for warmth) or tied shut with several short thongs (for better air circulation). The short fringes at the bottom of the sleeves and body may be cut into the material itself, but are usually separate pieces (as shown for the sleeve) that are sewn on after completion. Triangular flaps hang down both front and back. They are sewn across the top only. Generally, these were painted with red or yellow pigment and edged with beadwork, cloth, or strips of fur, along with leather pieces for fringe as on the sleeves. Sometimes lines of contrasting colors were carefully painted next to the beaded edging on the sleeves and flaps.

Koon-Kah-Za-Chy, or Protector of his Lodge, known in English as Apache John, head chief of the Kiowa-Apache tribe in Oklahoma. His clothing is of typical Southern Plains style, long twisted fringes decorating his buckskin shirt and leggings, along with plumes and small feathers. Otter fur was used for his braid wraps, legbands, and hangings for the wooden war club in his left hand, under the eagle tail feathers. His scarf has a tie slide made of German silver. He also wears around his neck a peace medal and a rosary, along with a bandolier of mescal beans, items that proclaim his political role and his religious affiliations. The horned headdress with straight-up eagle feathers is typical of his tribe, as are the legging flaps with their bead and brass button decorations.

Rodman Wannamaker photo taken in 1909

Shoulder Coverings

Vests and capes were worn in summer over the bare skin and in colder times over a cloth shirt when a jacket would be too cumbersome. Both kinds of coverings were commonly worn with old-time dance outfits, and capes are still a basic dress item for many dancers today. Powwow outfits in the Northern Plains area, for instance, often center on a decorated cape and matching aprons.

Vests

Native vests were originally copied from the vests of the invading culture. In fact, manufactured cloth vests (gambler's vests) were quite popular with men when "dressing for town" during the latter part of the nineteenth and early twentieth century. Older conservative men on many reserves today still wear dark cloth vests and black scarves for their daily dress.

Cloth vests can be bought cheaply at thrift stores. They can be decorated with beadwork or with ribbons sewn along the edges. Elk teeth and cowrie shells were commonly drilled and hung in rows to partially or fully cover cloth vests.

Leather vests can be made of buckskin or of heavier hide such as moose. They should be backed with colorful calico cloth for beauty, extra warmth, and comfort, and to keep thinner leather from stretching out of shape. If the lining is cut slightly larger than the vest, it can be folded over the outside to make a nice edging. It is best to cut the lining to shape as it is being sewn down, rather than beforehand, for the leather vest may stretch as you are sewing. Vests should be cut to fit loosely. For a pattern, use a cloth vest that fits you or make one out of paper. Begin sewing the three pieces together at the shoulders, and end up by sewing the sides down to the bottom. Add tie strings in front to complete the basic vest. Beadwork makes beautiful decoration on vests. Some of the finest examples of traditional art in beadwork were seen on many of the old-time, fully beaded vests. The Eastern tribes, who lived in the woods, preferred

The dentalium shell decorations on this blue cloth vest make it a simple but attractive work of art. These yellowish tooth-like shells are now quite rare and valuable, being also used on chokers and to decorate women's dresses. The vest is unlined, but edged in red patterned calico.

Photograph courtesy of Museum of the Plains Indian

profuse designs of connecting flowers and leaves for their vests (as well as most other beadwork). The People who lived on the wide-open Plains used intricate geometric designs with straight lines done in lazy-stitch style to decorate their vests. The People of the Northern Plains and Mountains also used geometric designs in appliqué style but preferred simple designs of colorful flowers and leaves.

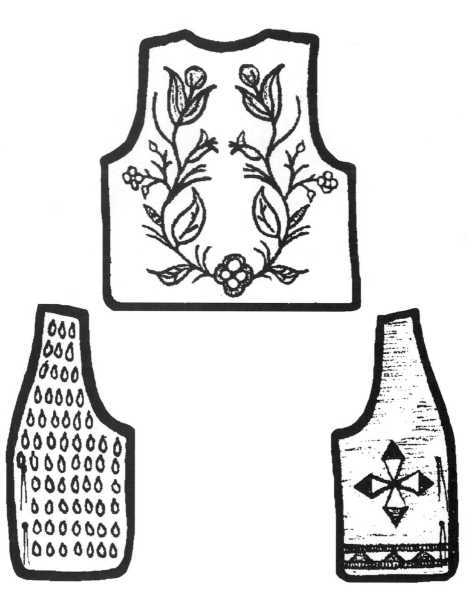

Stunning would be a good description of this fully beaded Blackfoot vest with its intricate floral design. This is northern style appliqué beadwork at its finest, made around 1900, when traditional art like this really flourished. Note that sequins are sewn over the beadwork in rows, adding a further luster to the final result.

Photograph courtesy of Museum of the Plains Indian

Capes

Capes of fringed leather (A) were a basic part of the long ago clothing worn in the Eastern Woodlands. For dancing and special occasions, these People made capes of dark velvet—heavily beaded with floral designs (B)—which were a part of elaborate, matching outfits.

Skins of animals such as otter, bobcat, and coyote were often slit down the middle so that they could be worn over the shoulders for warmth and appearance, as well as for spiritual power. The skins were left intact, often lined, and worn with the animal's head on the chest and the tail down the back. Sometimes mirrors or other decorations were sewn to the skins; other times Medicine items were attached.

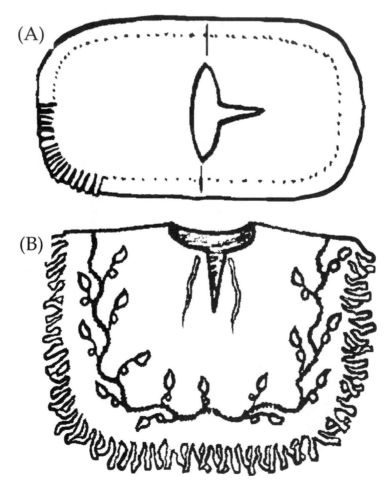

(A)

(B)

Men's Leggings

When the People were given government rations and presents in the old days, they generally went home and reworked many of the useful things to suit their own needs. Metal utensils were often cut up and made into knives, arrowheads, or armbands. Shoes and boots had their tops cut off and used for wristguards and such—while the buttons were sewn onto other things for decoration. Trousers were turned into leggings by having the crotch cut out of them—a practice which some old-timers continued well into the present century.

The use of crotchless pants appears to be quite ancient. It is believed that many of the Northern tribes used leggings long before adopting

Everyday clothing for Salish-Flathead People at the beginning of the 1900s still included leggings and breechcloths for men, long dresses for women, and long hair for both. Also common was the wearing of scarves around the neck and blankets around the waist or over the shoulders. The men's leggings are of typical northern style with decorated panels around the bottoms; one pair is made from plain wool cloth, the other from a multistriped blanket. Somewhat unusual for People of the Rocky Mountain region are the bare feet of the old man at the left and his little grandson (the one who is trying to tease the little girl held by her mom).

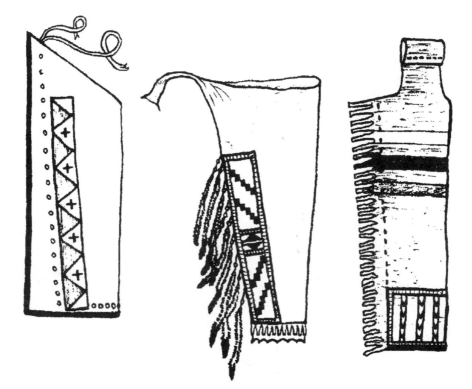

breechcloths and shirts. Even in winter they wore only moccasins, leggings, and a buffalo robe. The leggings provided warmth, as well as protection from brush and brambles. After breechcloths gave way to full pants, many men still wore leggings in the winter time. Slipped over regular pants, your leggings will really keep those cold winds from biting through!

In the long ago, deerskin and elkskin leggings were worn in the summertime, while buffalo or other skins (with the fur turned inward) were used for winter leggings. The skin leggings were made like hollow tubes that covered the legs from the ankles to the thighs, where they were tied to the belt with thongs. They generally had fringes or wide flaps along the seams down the outside. Often they were also fringed around the bottoms, and sometimes the fringes, or side-flaps, trailed for a foot or two on the ground behind. Decoration consisted mainly of painting—either stripes, spiritual designs, war deeds, or solid colors covering the whole leggings—and long, narrow strips of quill work in front of, and parallel with, the seams.

With the coming of blankets and beads, leggings were often made of wool, and the decorations consisted mainly of beadwork. These wool leggings had flaps of varying widths which stood out and away from the legs. Beaded strips were done on separate material and then sewn to the main part of the legging, just ahead of the seam. Another style of decoration that was used widely—especially by the tribes of the Northern Plains area—was the beaded panel. Panels consisted of rectangular pieces of thin wool or velvet, usually four to six inches high and long enough to go either all the way or half way around the bottom of the tube part of the legging. These cloth panels were backed with stiff material, covered with beadwork (fully or partially—often the color of the cloth served as a background) and sewn to the bottom of the legging.

To make a pair of leggings, you will need two average hides or one blanket. The front and back of each legging is cut out as one piece, then sewn, laced, or tied together along a straight line drawn at an angle from the large part of the leg at the top to the narrow part at the ankle. The flaps will be narrow at the top and wide at the bottom. They are left open, not sewn together. If you wish more warmth or don't like wool next to your skin, cut some calico material about one-half wider all around than your legging pieces, and sew this on before closing up your leggings. Fold the extra material around to the front and stitch it down neatly, and you will have a nice trim all around. Also, the inside of your flaps can be quite flashy this way. Sew cloth loops or leather thongs to the front side of each legging so that the leggings hang properly when fastened onto your belt.

A Southwest style of legging is knee-high and made from thick hide. It is tied on at the calf with sashes. It was worn out in the deserts as protection from cactus, brush, and snake bites.

81

Ute Skin Leggings

The leggings in the drawing on this page are the old style worn by men of the Ute tribe of Colorado. They are typical of leggings worn by other tribes on the Southern Plains and in the Southwest. Each legging is made from one deer hide. These are cut as shown in the drawing on the lower right, folded in half along the center line, and sewn up as far as the out-side dotted lines. The separate piece with the ragged edges in the lower left corner of the drawing was commonly sewn to the inside bottom of the leg tubes so that it would protrude beyond the bottom fringe. When wear-ing, this piece covered the moccasins, the fringe trailed on the ground, and the legging was tied to a belt by the two pieces extending from the top. Beaded strips were applied as shown. Bells, deer hooves, pieces of hair and fur, and other small things were attached to the strips, fringes, and wherever else the wearer wished to have them.

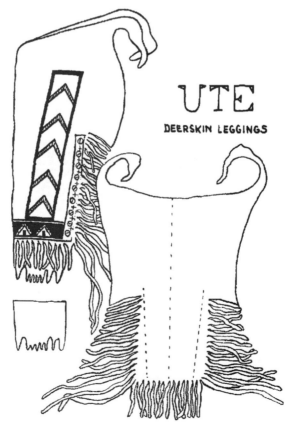

UTE
DEERSKIN LEGGINGS

Breechcloths

In the warm summertime a breech-cloth held up by a soft leather thong is often all the clothing necessary for physical pleasure with minimum security. This has long been the favorite style of Native dress in warm areas and warm times. Warriors preferred it when going into battle, for it allowed their bodies free movement. Young boys of most tribes seldom wore anything else while playing in warm weather. Among a number of tribes, even girls wore breechcloths before they reached the age of puberty.

A breechcloth is a piece of skin or cloth that is seldom more than a foot wide, and is passed between the legs, up over the belt, and left to hang down in front and behind. The softest tanning

was required for those made of skin to help avoid chafing. Blue wool trade-cloth was favored for warmth and comfort after it became available. Breechcloths were generally worn plain; those of skin were often fringed. Cloth breechcloths for dress were decorated with colored ribbons and metal sequins, which were generally sewn on in many parallel lines or combinations of lines and Vs. Circles and crosses were made with sequins, and sometimes beadwork was added. Breechcloth lengths varied—from barely covering to tails that hung down to the ground.

Tribes in the East and in some other areas wore aprons instead of breechcloths. These were just leather or cloth flaps that hung down from a belt in front and behind. Sometimes they were just tied together at the sides and worn without a belt. Some of them were beautifully decorated with floral designs done in appliqué beadwork.

Here is about the least that one could wear and still be considered to have on "traditional dress." This man is Left-Handed, a Salish-Flathead, standing beside his partly opened summer tipi in 1907. His long breechcloth is made from a tartan shawl of the kind that ladies in those times wore around their necks in cold weather. This is held up by a hidden buckskin thong, while over the top there is a bead and tack-decorated panel belt with a long, split, tack-decorated drop. He also has on a loop necklace with strands of round white beads, plus a pair of conch shells for earrings.

F.E. Peeso photo—Butte, Montana

Black-Tailed Deer, a Ute, as he appeared during an official visit to Washington, D.C. in 1868. The silver spot over the forehead was an old life symbol for warriors—his war exploits are drawn on the flaps of his "war leggings." A handy mirror is partly covered by his little pouch of paints and sundries.

Photo from Bureau of American Ethnology

Necklaces and Earrings

Like an artist with an empty canvas, the old-time individual loved to decorate any exposed areas of his body. These were places to present calling cards—necklaces with mystifying little pouches, breastplates of fine, polished bones, beadwork to exclaim artistic talent, or strings of animal claws to testify for the wearer's prowess.

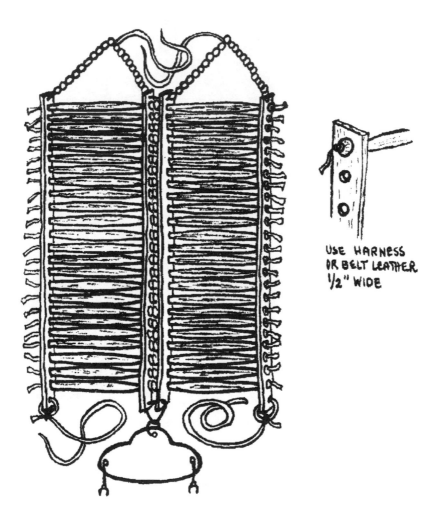

USE HARNESS
OR BELT LEATHER
½" WIDE

Breastplates

Though an occasional arrow must have been deflected by the hard, little bone "hairpipes" worn on breastplates during old-time battles, these served basically as items of beauty, not as pieces of armor. The hairpipes are made from deer leg bones (in factories, not by hand—they have long been an important part of traders' stocks) and  strung up in various ways to hang over the chest. Some long breastplates reached from the neck down past the waist, while others were barely six inches long, hanging like white chevrons from their thongs around the neck.

Hairpipes have always been costly. Many dancers today buy imitation bone pipes or make their own from bird and animal bones or corncob pipe stems. Long hairpipes (three inches or more) are generally worn in two parallel rows, while shorter pipes are often mounted in three, or even four rows—the length depending on desire and money.

Lay your hairpipes out in the way you wish to mount them. The drawing on page 86 shows a "typical" example. Use soft thongs to string the pipes between tough, but pliable, leather straps. Old harness leather, found in a corner of your barn, works well for such purposes. One strap goes on each side of the breastplate, and two go down the middle, with large necklace, or "Crow" style beads, strung in the center. With really long hairpipes only one strap and no beads may be used down the center. At the top of the completed plate is a pair of thongs that tie around the waist.

A couple of young Lakota-Sioux men dressed neatly for a city visit around 1910. Both have blankets, used instead of jackets. They also both wear cloth leggings and beaded moccasins. At left is Medicine Horse, wearing an otterskin chestpiece decorated with round mirrors, and his hair loose. Plenty Horse, at right, has a hairpipe breastplate with a symbolic wheel attached. His hair is tied in two short bunches, with an eagle plume tied at top to indicate a special ceremony he has gone through.

Shells are an important part of traditional Flathead clothing, the mountain tribe being closely related to the Salish People on the West Coast. Flathead tribal leader Victor Vanderburg is seen here outside his tipi in 1907, wearing an unusually thick pair of wire earring hoops and large conch shells. Also, his loop necklace is made up of tiny shell beads strung on cords and held at the sides by a pair of leather strips decorated with tiny seed beads; his dark shirt is of velvet. His long hair is wrapped with strips of otter skin, while round mirrors decorate a strip of the same fur that he wears across his chest as a bandolier.

Photograph by F.E. Peeso—Butte, Montana

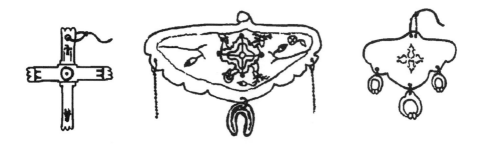

Some item was often attached to the bottom center of a breastplate. Little bunches of ermine tails, a large coin, or a small pouch of Medicine paint or herb were common items. The drawing on page 86 shows a "pectoral" worn there. These items were taken from or copied after early Spanish horse gear and were often made on the Plains from trade metal, such as German "silver." Large, Christian-style crosses were made and used the same way. Scenes and designs were often scratch-engraved on pectorals and crosses—pictographs of battle exploits and designs with spiritual meaning were most common. Sometimes these metal items were worn on a thong like a necklace, but more often they were fastened to the bottoms of breastplates. Chains and little metal crescents and designs were attached to holes drilled into the pectorals.

Southern Ute chief Buckskin Charley and his wife, both in their finest tribal style of traditional dress as worn in the Colorado Rockies around 1900. She has on a long cloth dress with open, wing-like sleeves, the bottom of it decorated with ribbons and sequins. The silver conch belt around her waist was obtained in trade from neighbors, as was the fringed, flowered shawl that she has draped over one shoulder and part-way around her waist.

Husband and wife both wear their long hair in two parts, hers braided, his wrapped with long strips of cloth. They also share the same style chokers, made of long glass tube beads, and their moccasins are beaded. His shirt is fringed and decorated with a cross of silver buttons. The leather leggings are also fringed, with the long bottom trailers that distinguish Utes. He carries a feather fan in one hand and holds a staff in the other, possibly a symbol of being chief. The single feather worn at the back of his head signified that he had killed enemies in battle.

A loop necklace of white glass disc beads, which fully covers his chest, is among the highlights of this young Crow man's traditional clothing. It is edged by a pair of tack-decorated leather strips, each with a round conch shell near the top. A smaller conch shell is also attached to the front of his bead and cowrie shell choker. The white beaded cuffs are decorated with colorful floral designs, and a striped Pendelton blanket is draped over his shoulders. His three-braid "warrior" hair style is especially popular among the Blackfoot People and their eastern neighbors, the Crows.

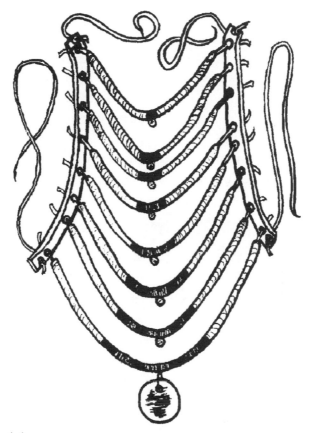

Loop Necklaces

The drawing above shows the basic style for the loop necklaces that were more popular than breastplates in the Northern Plains area. Some tribes, like the Crow and the Flathead, preferred small "disc" beads (looking like bone washers) strung on loops of buckskin, while others, such as the Blackfoot and Sarcee, wrapped tiny seed beads round and round on the buckskin loops with thread. Still others strung large necklace beads or short hairpipes on the loops.

The most difficult part of making the loop necklace is obtaining enough beads to string up. After you have done this, cut the number of buckskin thongs you wish to use—usually eight to twelve. These get progressively longer as they go down. They are strung to harness leather straps on each side and knotted on the ends. Buckskin tie strings are used to tie around the neck and waist.

Earrings

Most Native People had their ears pierced at an early age. Among some tribes this was done in a ceremonial manner; among others it was done simply by the mother at home. Long ago, a greased porcupine's quill, a cactus spine, or a sharpened twig was thrust through the earlobe and broken off close to the surface. In later times, a piece of sinew or buckskin thong was pulled through with a needle, or an open ring was pressed against the lobe and left to wear out an opening by constant pressure.

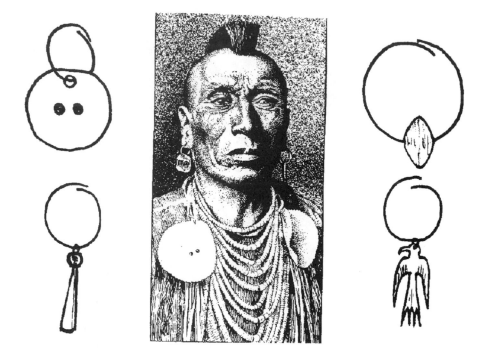

Each lobe generally had one hole. However, some People, like the Comanche and Wichita, thought it fashionable to have a number of holes up along the outside of the ears, and to wear a small earring in each.

Silver wires were preferred for earrings. Some tribes, like the Utes, often wore only large, heavy hoops made from wires. Round pieces of shell were popularly worn from small or large hoops. Sometimes whole shells or pieces of shell carved into shapes were hung from wire hoops. In the same way, silver and glass beads were worn on hoops. The Sioux

94

Southern Ute People in "modernized," everyday clothing. Notice the different styles of earrings. The clothes of the men were store-bought, those of the women sewn by hand. In later tipi days, treadle sewing machines were sometimes seen inside lodges.

prized earrings made of dentalium shells, strung in rows like the chokers, and tied to the wire hoops. Ball and cone earrings were made by hanging a metal head and a tin cone from the wire hoop. Members of the Native American Church often wear symbols of their religion on earrings today.

The silversmiths and jewelry workers of the Southwest tribes produce earrings and necklaces of a very artistic type. This craft was influenced by Mexicans and Spaniards, and the products have long been eagerly sought by members of other tribes. Their manufacture, however, requires more knowledge and material than the general reader of these words will easily find.

A Comanche leader of the Southern Plains named Mow-way shows a combination of store-bought shirt and vest with traditional items like the large silver concho used for a tie slide, possibly in honor of the sun, and also the grizzly claw in his hair, which had to do with spiritual powers. He may have cut his hair to mourn the loss of someone in his family.

Ready for a hot summer day powwow, this man of the Spokane tribe was photographed around 1910. Ten strands of disc beads make up the loop necklace that covers part of his chest, over which he wears a much longer necklace with alternating strands of glass beads, brass beads, and long tubular hairpipes, the sections divided from each other by dark strips of leather. His choker is similarly made with shorter hairpipes and beads. In his earlobes he wears large wire hoops with drilled conch shell pendants. A pair of shiny brass bands decorate his upper arms. His leather belt is decorated with alternating panels of seed beads and brass tacks, as in the long drop on his left side. The decorated belt is worn over the top of a wool breechcloth, which is held up by a hidden thong around his waist. The woolen leggings have bead-decorated panels at the bottom and fringed panels on the sides, in typical Northern Plains and Rockies style. He has followed a custom used by warriors of the past—along with dancers on hot days—which was to untie the leggings from the belt at the top, letting them drop down and gather below his knees. His long hair is pulled back with a porcupine and deer hair roach tied at the top. That white thing attached to the roach could be an eagle plume blowing in the wind or his girlfriend's silk kerchief. Tied to the peeled stick that he's got standing from the ground is his bustle and feather belt. The light colored fur strips decorated by round mirrors and a few eagle tail feathers was either a neck ornament or a bandolier. The bustle part of the top has a variety of feathers strung up in circles. We are left to wonder why his beaded and fringed pipe bag is hanging at center bottom of this unusual item, nor is it clear what sort of decorated dance stick he is carrying in his left hand.

Other Necklaces and Chokers

Most any material that suits your fancy can, of course, be strung up and worn as a necklace. Claws were usually attached to a heavy thong, which was run through holes drilled at the base of the claws. Smaller holes were then drilled at the halfway point of the claws so that a strip of sinew could be run through to give the necklace more rigidity. Pieces of fur can be folded over the two thongs and sewn together for added appearance.

Long necklaces were sometimes worn as bandoleers—hung over one shoulder and under the other arm. They were strung with seeds, beads, deer hooves, gun shells, and other fancy or noisy items. Necklaces, like everything else, were worn for appearance as well as for personal spiritual reasons.

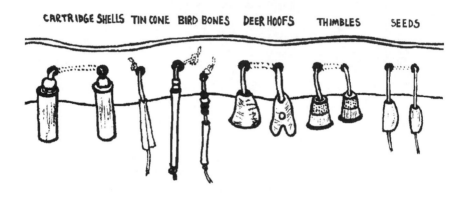

CARTRIDGE SHELLS TIN CONE BIRD BONES DEER HOOFS THIMBLES SEEDS

Chokers worn around the throat were also of many kinds—some that could be worn all the time, others that were impressive but so fragile or awkward that they were worn for special occasions only. The tribes of the Plains area seem to have used chokers much more than others. The Sioux People preferred the tusk-like dentalium shells for theirs, strung in rows on buckskin thongs with leather strips and brass beads for spacers. They also liked to string up short hairpipes this way. Glass tube beads were similarly strung up and worn as chokers among many tribes. Everyday chokers were commonly made up of one to two strands of necklace beads. The Blackfoot People often strung elk teeth or cowrie shells between the beads. Strips of beadwork were sometimes worn as chokers. Some later-day dance outfits were complete with a choker that was patterned after the common high collar and tie, but was made of buckskin and fully

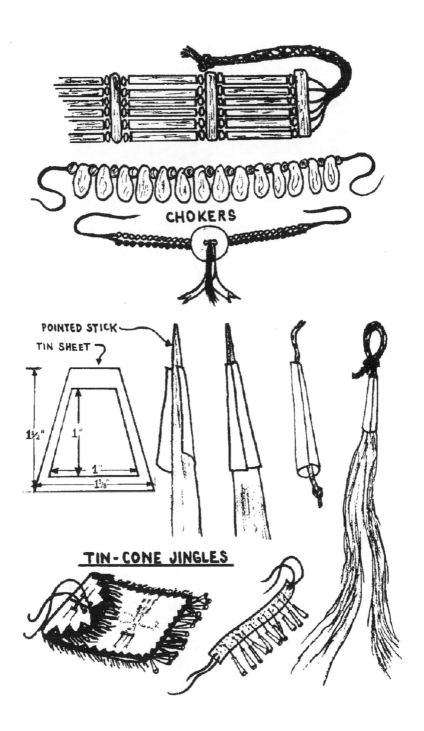

CHOKERS

POINTED STICK

TIN SHEET

1½"
1"
1"
1⅜"

TIN-CONE JINGLES

beaded. Shells, metal items, and strips of fur were sometimes tied to chokers so that they would hang down in front. Chokers are most always tied behind the neck.

The old and new combine to give dignity to this San Carlos Apache chief named Josh, who was photographed at the Omaha Exposition in 1898.

Photograph by Rinehart

Long hair, recently unbraided and neatly brushed, was obviously a source of pride for this middle-aged chief of a Canadian Blackfoot band. His symbol of office is the gold-topped staff in his hand, presented to him by a queen's representative, which he carries along with his tab-edged pipe bag. The weasel-decorated buckskin shirt is another symbol of leadership, its power and songs ceremonially transferred from one person to the next in a sacred ritual. Weasels on his leggings indicate that they were part of the sacred outfit too, even though they are of wool instead of the customary buckskin used for this purpose.

Hair

The manners of wearing the hair were many and varied—but most People in the Old Days allowed their hair to grow naturally long. The desire for individual expression, too, can be fulfilled in a number of ways in and about the hair. And finally, present-day hair specialists claim that hair cropped close to the scalp falls out at a rate of more than ten times that of waist-length hair.

Hair Styles

The following list describes some of the ways that various Native American People wore their hair. Some individuals always wore their hair in the same way; others changed styles often. Members of some tribes copied and adopted hair styles generally considered to be specifically from some other tribe. Personal dreams and tastes, as well as tribal traditions, determined the style of hair worn.

1. Hair worn loose and long—This is certainly the basic style of wearing long hair. It was the common style for Apache men, who often wore wide cloth bands around their heads to keep the hair back. It was a common style for men of the Mojave tribe, who just wore it straight clown. It was also a common style for men and women of the Pacific Northwest, who kept the hair out of their eyes when working with a headband of fur or skin. Individuals who normally wore their hair in one of the dressed styles often wore their hair loose for ceremonial occasions, such as Vision Seeking and Sun Dancing, to obtain a more complete feeling of freedom and flowing with All. The hair was generally parted in the center or on the side when it was worn this way. This was also one of two styles used most commonly by Native women.

2. Hair worn loose and cropped—Among some tribes the men usually wore their hair shoulder-length and kept it always cropped that way. The Messiah-of-the-Ghost-Dance, the

The traditional dress of a head chief. Clean white tipis and the towering Rocky Mountains make an appropriate backdrop for this portrait of Salish-Flathead Chief Charlo, standing with his wife and granddaughter on their western Montana reservation about 1900. His clothing would have been similar 30 or 40 years earlier, when he might have set out on one of his war trails looking about like this. His long hair is worn loose down over his striped cloth shirt and hairpipe breastplate, which was originally meant to help deflect arrows. There's a Pendelton blanket wrapped around his waist, and on his right arm is a feather-decorated shield. His wife has on her buckskin dress, which she probably tanned and sewed herself. The little girl is wearing a cloth dress decorated with cowrie shells, plus a necklace with a big round conch shell. In her hand she carries a decorated bag woven by a neighboring tribe from corn husks.

Paiute named Wovoka, wore his hair this way. Kiowa and Sac and Fox men liked this style. Widows and mourners of many tribes generally hacked their hair off to shoulder length to show their grief.

3. Hair worn long with bangs—This style was commonly used on children to keep the hair out of the face. The Pueblo tribes of the Southwest have been particularly fond of bangs. Long ago, men on the Plains sometimes cut a small "forelock" short and let it hang over their foreheads and noses.

4. Hair worn back—

   a. For practical reasons many individuals used buckskin thongs to simply tie their hair behind their heads.

   b. Some wore their hair in one braid down the back. Married Iroquois women wore one braid doubled up and tied with buckskin.

   c. Another style consisted of a number of braids made after the hair was combed back. The braids were then tied together into one bunch.

   d. The People in the Southwest still comb their long hair back and roll it up in a queue, then wrap it with cloth. The Navajo wear it this way; Navajo men usually wear a wide band of cloth around the head also. Hopi men wear the back of their hair in this fashion. They crop the sides shoulder length and often cut bangs above the eyes. For ceremonies they wear all their hair loose.

5. Hair worn in two braids at the sides—

   a. With a part down the center, one braid on each side covering the ears. This is the other basic style for the majority of Native women, many of whom still wear their hair this way. They often tie the braids together and throw them behind while working. This is also the most common old-time style among the People of the Plains and many neighboring areas. Sioux and Cheyenne men favored it, Chippewa men to the east used it, and many Buffalo/Plains-oriented men and women living in Pueblo villages of the

Southwest also wore their hair in the handsome, two-braid, center part style.

b. A similar style differed in leaving the ears uncovered. This was done by some for comfort, by others because they lacked enough hair to cover the ears properly. Men more often did this than women.

c. Another similar style differed in having the part off to one side. This was the common men's style on and near the Northern Plains.

d. Parted on one side with a lock cut shorter in front—The lock was combed and trained to lay to one side and cover the hair that went into the braids, though it often ended up hanging into the face.

e. A similar style was used by some men—The lock was left long enough to be gathered from the forehead back into a bunch and then tied to the rest of the hair at the crown with a buckskin thong. This lock covered the part and was usually gathered loose enough to form a slight pompadour over the forehead. It was a favorite style among Flathead men.

f. In a similar style, the lock was cut from two to six inches long, coated with bear grease or buffalo dung, and trained to stand straight up over the forehead. It was an identifying style of Crow men, though it was also worn by a few men of neighboring tribes—notably Chief Joseph of the Nez Perce and Weasel Tail of the Blackfoot tribe.

g. Another variation worn by men with two braids at the sides left a third section of hair hanging loose down the neck.

6. Hair worn in three braids—

a. The favorite style among Blackfoot men was to divide the hair into three even parts for braiding. Two braids were made high at each side in front of the ears, and another hung down the back. Less often the braids at the sides covered the ears. Sometimes the side part was used with this style; more often it was worn with the long lock tied back.

This elderly Cree man of the late 1800s no doubt got great pleasure—and admiration—from his four thick braids of long hair. All the more so since, no doubt, a few of his enemies in decades past were looking for ways to take one or two of those braids back home for trophies. He has a rolled-up black scarf tied around his head, so it's hard to tell just what his hair stylist did up there. (Men like this traditionally had their wives or daughters work their hair.) It was a traditional custom among some warriors of the past to paste horse hair or the combed-out hair of other persons into their own in order to lengthen it. One famous Crow chief named Long Hair was documented to have thirty-six feet of tresses, but close inspection showed his own hair to be much shorter than that. The choker is of brass beads, while the capote is a white trade blanket.

b. Another three-braid style seen among many tribes really consisted of two main braids and a thin "scalplock" down the back. This was a warrior's hair style from the Old Days, worn to tempt the enemy. If the wearer was knocked down or slain in battle, the first enemy to reach him usually grabbed the braided scalplock, put one of his feet on the victim's head, and gave a swift, curving slash with his knife, neatly severing the braid and skin to which it was attached. Wounded men often survived this "scalp-lift." The victor scraped the skin clean, then laced his little symbol tightly to a small willow hoop and took it back to camp to represent the slain warrior. During the Victory Dance, war widows often danced with the scalps, then flung them into the fire to signify that the past was now over.

7. Hair worn in several braids—Two braids at each side and sometimes one more in back was another style sometimes used in the old days, particularly among Northern tribes like the Crees. Rarely, a man might have a number of braids all around his head, generally in fulfillment of a Dream.

8. Hair worn straight up—An old-time warrior's style used for its grotesque effect. The Chippewa, when going to war, tied the thin scalplock with stiff material at its base, so that it stood straight up for several inches, while the rest of the hair fell back down loosely like a water fountain. Others did this with all their hair. Still others mixed grease or buffalo dung into their hair and made it stand up in a huge point or curve back like a horn. Often this projection was smeared with paint. Kutenai warriors used a bunch of tule reeds as a base to tie their hair up to.

9. Hair worn in a knot on the head—This was a religious hair style, used primarily by the sacred Medicine Pipe Men of the Blackfoot tribe. The knot was usually worn over the forehead with braids at the sides and back. Individuals who were totally devoted to their spiritual leadership often put all their hair into one braid, which was then coiled and

fastened to protrude above the forehead. Sacred paint generally covered the hair.

10. Hair worn long down the center of the head—The well-known "Mohawk" style. This was a common style for men among many East Coast tribes, as well as some tribes in other areas, such as the Pawnee of the Eastern Plains. The hair on the sides of the head was generally plucked (yes, plucked!) out, and only a narrow strip down the center was allowed to grow long. This was sometimes worn in a braid down the back.

Hair Care

The Bishop of Meaux long ago observed of the Native People:

"They are certainly fond of their hair, and they would consider themselves disgraced if any part of it was cut off. To preserve their hair they grease it often and powder it with the dust of spruce bark, and sometimes with vermillion: then they wrap it up in the skin of an eel or serpent..."

The trader Alexander Henry said this about the Blackfoot men whom he saw:

"The young men allow theirs (hair) to flow loose and lank about their necks, taking great care to keep it smooth about the face... the elder men allow their hair to grow, and twist it... they wear it on the forehead, projecting seven or eight inches in a huge knob, smeared with red Earth."

The anthropologist Clark Wissler found, even after the turn of the century, that they still "spend a great deal of their time brushing and caring for their hair. They admire long hair and use charms to increase its length." Buffalo hair and hair collected from mourners was often attached to the end of the hair with spruce gum for added length. There is belief among Native People that hair holds wisdom, thus those with hair cut short are considered somewhat unwise.

Though Native People had body and face hair, most of them kept all exposed hair plucked, save that on the head. Many men kept handmade

Chief John Hunter and his wife were members of the Stoney tribe, living in the Canadian Rockies near Banff National Park. They were photographed on horseback in the 1940s, riding in a parade through the famous resort town of Banff. He is dressed humbly for a chief, with only the peace medal on its gold chain indicating his leader status. He wears a buckskin vest with beaded flowers over his smoked buckskin jacket, plus a striped piece of cloth for a headband. His hair is in the most common style used by men of Plains tribes—two braids—although he has also cut a forelock that falls down towards his eyes.

metal tweezers fastened to a necklace or pouch and spent much time seeking stray hair and plucking it out. Facial hair grew thicker among some tribes than others, so that mustaches and even beards were commonly seen in some areas. The men along the Pacific Coast, for instance, regularly wore full mustaches and sometimes long goatees. Buckskin Charley, a Ute Chief from Colorado, was known for his mustache, which curled down around his mouth. A number of Flathead men trained mustaches and even waxed the ends. Names like Hairy Face and Bearded One were heard occasionally among tribes on the Plains.

Combs were not known in the Old Days, but the hair was often brushed. A primitive brush consisted of a handful of flexible twigs, bound together with buckskin. The most common brush on the Plains was made by inserting a stick of wood into a porcupine's tail. A handful of horse hair was sometimes bound and doubled over to make a soft hair brush.

Hair tonics and washes were prepared by the Native People from various plants which grew in their areas. Cactus suds were commonly used by the Hopi and others in the Southwest. Sweet grass, which was widely used as a sacred incense, was also boiled in water and used as a hair tonic. Sometimes it was mixed with cedar leaves or other plants for aroma and medicinal effect. The common bear grass was often boiled and used to control falling hair.

Head Wear

Numerous things were worn over, in, and around the hair. Headbands of buckskin or strips of fur were worn, especially during the winter, by both men and women (though not as commonly as one might think). Winter hats of fur, whole animal skins, and even bird skins were popular everywhere. Woven hats (made like baskets) were worn by women of many basket-weaving tribes. Eye shades were made from rectangular pieces of rawhide with head-holes cut out of them.

Men often wore head coverings that identified their tribal roles or spiritual powers. Feather bonnets and single feathers, worn in back, top, or front of the head, generally represented war deeds. Headdresses with horns, worn with caps of buffalo fur, ermine skins, or feather bonnets, often signified membership in a society or power as a Medicine Man.

Personal Medicine items were quite often attached to the hair—especially during hunting or war expeditions. Animal claws, bird feathers and parts, and sacred little pouches were common.

Silver conchos were tied into the hair, often to the small scalplock in back. Some men tied leather straps to their hair that were covered with conchos (like belts), often reached the ground, and weighed many pounds.

Thongs with beads were often tied into the hair above each temple and allowed to dangle in front of the eyes. Beaded headbands were uncommon in most areas, and "princess headbands" were invented by non-Natives, along with the term that gives them their name.

Fancy young men among the Sioux commonly wore a feather ornament in back of their heads that consisted of one or more upright eagle feathers, a strip of bead or quill work, and the tail of a bull hanging down behind. Their Blackfoot counterparts often wore an item down their backs that was made from a number of long strands of human hair joined by pieces of gum and otherwise decorated.

Scarves and hats of every kind were worn by both men and women after their introduction. Hats were commonly worn as they came from the factory—with flat brims and rounded crowns. Feathers and scarves were two of the most common hat decorations.

Men and women of many tribes have enjoyed wearing European hats as part of their traditional clothing for the past couple hundred years, often shaping and decorating these in their own distinctive manner. This 1920s photo shows Weasel Rider, also known as Alec Nanna, a noted Kutenai from Elmo, Montana. Weasels were among his special animals, as he wears strips of their fur on the crown of his hat and as hair drops. In addition, strips of otter fur decorate his long hair, while a woolen trade blanket covers his shoulders. He had a half-breed friend named Eagle Feathers, or Abel Gravelle, among the Canadian Kutenai. In keeping with an unusual tribal custom, the two of them agreed to share the same wife, a fine-looking woman named Cecile. She had one child who became a noted tribal elder named Ambrose Gravelle and was said to have shown traits from both his fathers.

Hileman Photo—Glacier Studio Collection

Scarves are very functional items that were eagerly acquired in the Old Days. Mainly, of course, they were tied around the neck, the ends hanging down the front or back. Some People just tied a double knot and let the ends hang loose, while others used tie slides made of silver, buckskin, or animal vertebrae, and tied the ends into knots too. In warm weather, thin scarves of cotton or ones made from calico material were used. In cold weather, heavier material was used, and more than one scarf was often worn. One might be tied around the neck, another one tied behind the neck so that it could be pulled up in front to cover the mouth and nose in an icy cold, and still another might be worn over the head, peasant style, to protect the ears and the sides of the face. Men often wore scarves on their heads beneath fur hats in this way. The most common style of headband, especially in the Southwest country, was made by rolling up a scarf and tying it behind. Women usually wore scarves in the manner of caps—covering the head and tied behind.

Fur hats of very primitive styles were being worn by these three old Stoney men when they paraded through the streets of Banff, Alberta, for a national park festival around 1950. Wearing the buffalo headdress with horns is noted Stoney philosopher and world traveller Walking Buffalo, whose published autobiography has sold numerous printings. Wearing a buffalo fur vest plus a wide, decorated belt of the same material makes him dressed as if illustrating his name. Stoneys are skilled mountain hunters, as symbolized by the man in the middle whose hat and bandoleer are both made from mountain goat fur. The man at right preferred his hat and belt made from deerhide with the hair left on, which certainly makes it eye-catching. The fringed shirts with various drawings and decorations were a style for warriors in the Old Days. The middle shirt is old and made of buckskin, while the other two are more recent copies made of muslin cloth. Possibly these three old friends decided they would show the modern world just once more how they and their forefathers dressed to live in harmony with nature. However, the hat on the right would sure shed rain and snow a lot better if its hair was pointing down instead of upwards.

Nicholas Morant Photo/Canadian Pacific Railway

Painting and Tattooing

Prince Maximilian, during his travels on the continent in the 1800s, made this observation:

> "They paint their faces red with vermillion: this colour, which they procure by barter from the traders, is rubbed in with fat, which gives them a shining appearance. Others colour only the edge of their eyelids, and some stripes in the face, with red; others use a certain yellow clay for the face and red round the eyes; others, again, paint the face red, arid forehead, a stripe down the nose, and the chin, blue, with the shining Earth from the Mountains . . . "

Little leather pouches filled with paint powders were often attached to articles of clothing or in the hair in the Old Days. Most People back then kept their paint applied as carefully as they kept their hair combed. And though men going to war often used grotesque designs and patterns in an attempt to frighten the enemy with their power, most painting was not considered "war paint." Many People made a daily practice of painting the part in their hair or the upper part of the cheek to add a highlight to their personal appearance. White clay was often used to coat the face skin if a day in the bright light of sun was planned, for many preferred light skin to that tanned dark by sunshine. People in mourning kept their faces, and sometimes their bodies and clothing, covered with black paint. And, for religious occasions, there were many reasons and methods of painting. Dreams, in fact, dictated most individual styles, while ceremonies and their functionaries always required traditional manners of painting. In such cases the pigment was called "sacred paint, " or "sacred Earth," and represented the spiritual presence and oneness with Mother Earth.

Complete "toilet kits" were kept in small, decorated pouches and bags which were often worn on belts or at the end of necklaces. Inside were little bags of the paints that the owner used, some wrapped-up tallow or fat, some shells or tiny stone bowls for mixing, and pointed sticks (often the carved and sharpened ends of antlers) used for applying some of their finer designs. Mirrors, of course, were added when they became available.

A young man of the Déné tribe from the Canadian Plains. He is wearing a blanket capote and metal choker, and is painted for adventure. The Déné are actually composed of a number of little-known tribes in the Canadian interior. Interestingly, the name Déné is also used by the Navajo to denote themselves. It means "The People."

When painting, the tallow was generally rubbed into the palm of one hand and some paint mixed with it. This mixture was then applied with the thumb and forefinger of the other hand or with a stick. In the case of sacred paints, any excess was rubbed on Medicine bundles and articles, and also on pipe stems, robes, and clothing or into the hair. Devout Medicine Men in the Old Days often had sacred paint caked on virtually everything they owned, and the fragrance of ceremonial incense always informed others of their presence.

Sacred paints were often gathered at special locations. Other paints were found or produced in the user's area. Red paints came from earths, clays, and rocks that were powdered. White came from chalk-like earths and from clays. Black was made from charcoal. Blue came from a dark blue mud. Blue and green were both made from boiling certain kinds of rotten woods. Green was also made from an algae. Yellow came from an earth and from buffalo gall stones. Some People travelled great distances to procure material for certain kinds of paint, which they then traded to others in their tribe or even to People of other tribes.

Tattooing was done to some degree by all tribes in the long ago. Most tribes gave up the practice sometime before the reservation period. Tattooing was sometimes done for beauty, but mostly it was dictated in dreams and had personal spiritual meaning. Many times it was merely a permanent style of face and body painting. Married couples sometimes tattooed similar designs on each other as part of spiritual vows. Individuals often tattooed some representation of their personal Medicine on themselves—often where it could not be seen by others.

The Bishop of Meaux made these comments about tattooing among Eastern tribes:

> "Many men make various figures all over their bodies, by pricking themselves, others only in some parts . . . This operation is not painful in itself . . . they begin by tracing on light skin, drawn very tight, the figure they intend to make, then they prick little holes close together with the fins of a fish, or with needles, all over these traces, so as to draw blood. Then they rub themselves with charcoal dust, and other colours, well ground

and powdered. These powders sink into the skin, and the colours are never effaced: but soon after the skin swells, and forms a kind of a scab, accompanied with inflammation."

The People of the Thompson tribe in British Columbia applied their tattooes with needles of bone, cactus spines, or other thorns, often tied in small bunches with their points close together. In later years they preferred a steel sewing needle and thread. They blackened the thread with powdered charcoal and drew it underneath the skin where the design had been drawn. A few of their tattooing and painting styles are illustrated in these drawings.

Index

120

Additional Books by
Adolf Hungrywolf

Indian Tribes of the Northern Rockies
Adolf Hungrywolf

A wealth of cultural information and history about tribes living in the Northern Rocky Mountains. Includes dozens of vintage photographs, maps, and reprints of original treaties.

0-913990-74-4 $9.95 / $14.95 Canada

Legends Told by The Old People of Many Tribes
Revised Edition
Adolf Hungrywolf

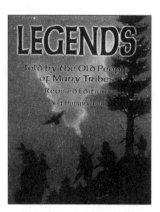

Now a new edition in an expanded format with new illustrations and stories. An inspired collection of special tales recorded from the Old People who heard them as children and passed them down. Gather your family around you and read them aloud.

0-913990-116-8 $9.95 / $14.95 Canada

Pow-wow Dancer's & Craftworker's Handbook
Adolf Hungrywolf

Powwow and dance costumes of the past 100 years displayed in color and black-and-white photographs, along with written histories and first-hand accounts of powwow activities. Descriptions of how to make traditional and modern powwow regalia are explained by text and pen and ink illustrations.

0-920698-62-X $24.95/ $37.95 Canada

Purchase these Native titles from your local bookstore, or you can buy them directly from:

Book Publishing Company
P.O. Box 99
Summertown, TN 38483

1-800-695-2241

Please include $3.95 per book for shipping and handling.

To find your Native books and products online, visit:

www.nativevoices.com